I AM RAYMOND WASHINGTON

ZACH FORTIER

WITH DERARD BARTON

steeleshark
press

I AM RAYMOND WASHINGTON

Published by
SteeleShark Press

ISBN-13: 978-0692359877
ISBN-10: 0692359877

Visit the author at:
Website: *www.zachfortier.com* and *www.bhcauthors.com*
Blog: *www.authorzachfortier.blogspot.com*
Facebook: *www.facebook.com/authorzach.fortier*
Twitter: *www.twitter.com/zachfortier1*
Goodreads: *www.goodreads.com/author/show/5164780.Zach_Fortier*

Purchase other books by Zach Fortier in print, eBook, or audio by scanning the QR code.

ALSO BY ZACH FORTIER

TABLE OF CONTENTS

PHOTO GALLERIES

RAYMOND LEE WASHINGTON BIO

BORN: August 14, 1953 in Los Angeles, California

MOTHER: Violet Samuel

FATHER: Raymond Washington, Sr.

BROTHERS: Ronald Joe, Donald Ray, Reggie, Derard

ADDRESS: 850 East 76th Street, Los Angeles, California

SCHOOLS:
Elementary—79th Street School
Junior High—Edison Junior High and Charles Drew Junior High
High School—Fremont, Washington, and Centennial

WORK HISTORY: Worked for the city of Los Angeles as a crew supervisor doing cleanup in the inner city for yards of the elderly, as well as for parks.

CHILDREN: Raymond had three daughters—Rayshana (Tammie), Lakeisha (Sonja), Shamika (Susie Edwards), and one son Raymond, Jr. (Peewee).

DIED: August 9, 1979 in Los Angeles, California from a gunshot fired at close range to the abdomen. Knew shooter and said he would take care of it when he healed. He never recovered. Raymond died that night approximately an hour and 20 minutes later. Was currently living at 6326 S. San Pedro, Apt #8 at the time of shooting.

ARREST RECORD: Arrested and convicted in California for robbery.

HOW IT ALL BEGAN

When I was first contacted by Cliff Woods—the nephew of Raymond Lee Washington[1]—and asked if I would be interested in writing a book about him, I asked, "Who the hell is Raymond Washington?" Cliff informed me that he was the man who founded the Crips in late 1969 as a fifteen or sixteen-year-old living in South Central Los Angeles. I thought, *Yeah right, everyone who is in the gang world knows that Stanley "Tookie" Williams was the founder of the set.* It was all over the media that Tookie was the founder, as the countdown to his very public execution began in the winter of 2005.[2]

I mentioned that to Cliff, and he asked that I look into it and *then* tell him what I thought. He believed there was a story that needed to be told. I admit, I was skeptical at best. If Tookie was not the founder, why did the entire national and world media credit him with being the founder and leader of the infamous Crips gang?

I started to look into Raymond Washington, first doing a Google search of his name, and later digging deep into the web looking for any real evidence to support or contradict Cliff's assertion. This journey began in the summer of 2012, and what I found was remarkable. Not only did I learn, without a doubt, that Raymond Washington was the sole founder of the Crips gang,[3] I also found out that there was an astounding amount of conflicting information about Raymond on the web. In some mainstream media, I found three different articles that each listed Raymond as being born in a different state.

When I looked into the origin of the name, "the Crips," I found so many different explanations of where the name had come from, I finally quit counting. It was ridiculous. I came across two sources with similar—albeit unfounded—stories. One was a law enforcement article that claimed one of the original gang members was shot and walked with a limp, and that was the reason for the name. *Time* magazine also published an article in 1975 stating the same thing.[4]

The article in *Time* was about a Piru gang member, Joseph "Bartender" Thomas, and his life in the Piru gang. He was killed shortly after the article was written. Here is an excerpt from the article that refers to Raymond and the origin of the Crips:

"But mainly the Piru plots, attacks and defends itself against its hated enemies, the local chapter of the Crips, which is perhaps the most vicious and largest street gang in the area. (The Crips got its name when its leader was shot in the leg and thereafter strutted around his turf with a cane.)"

One very common myth propagated by mainstream media is the idea that Raymond started the gang as the Baby Avenue Cribs, but because of his lack of education, or perhaps the inability of his fellow gang members to properly pronounce "crib," the name morphed into Crips. Perhaps this idea is popular because it implies that the Crips were a group of underachievers. Inner-city black kids who were less than the rest of us: less educated, less talented and lacking social skills, just less period. This might comfort the rank and file, nine to five, minivan driving, soccer mom crowd, but it does not represent the reality of the situation. Regardless of the reasons, it could not be further from the truth. The brutal reality is this: to survive in South Central Los Angeles during the time Raymond grew up (and perhaps still today) was the ultimate Darwinian test. Only the strongest, smartest, and most cunning survived. It was an environment that makes the current popular movies *The Hunger Games* and *Catching Fire* look like a vacation spent on *Gilligan's Island* with Skipper and Mary Ann. South Central is real, and the reality there is that it's a daily struggle to survive.

The myth of who Raymond Washington really was has grown exponentially since his death on the streets of Los Angeles in 1979. Unlike Stanley Williams, Raymond Washington did not die from an execution conducted by the criminal justice system. Raymond was drawn in by people he knew well, most likely friends or allies, and publicly executed on the streets he grew up on and later ruled. Much like the murder of Julius Caesar, Raymond was betrayed and murdered by one of his own.[5]

Raymond's murder has never been officially solved,[6] and is number eight in the top ten famous cases of unsolved murders and mysteries on *Listblogz.com*.[7] It is listed as the fourth biggest cold case/unsolved murder on *The Writers Forensics Blog*.[8]

I did eventually find out that it is well known on the street who called Raymond to a car that was familiar to him. Raymond approached, expecting a friend and ally. Instead he found a shotgun aimed at his abdomen and fired at point-blank range.

This is the life story of Raymond Lee Washington. The undisputed founder of one of the most notorious, deadly, and prolific gangs to ever dominate the streets of Los Angeles—the Crips.[9]

SPECIAL NOTE TO THE READER: In this biography, I have tried to withhold from passing any judgment on the life and deeds of Raymond Lee Washington, or, for that matter, the people who have agreed to talk to me about his life. I tried to remain as impartial as is possible for a writer with my background in law enforcement and gangs. This book is designed to give the reader the clearest possible picture of who Raymond Washington was and what made him unique. It is all here, everything I could find out, the good, the bad, and the incredibly ugly. No holds barred. My hope is that anyone reading this will be struck by an idea, or perhaps an epiphany that no other book has provided. I found stories about how cold and heartless Raymond could be to his enemies. These were tempered by almost unbelievable stories of compassion and patience. The duality of Raymond Washington was hard to make sense of, and finally, after many struggles with how to best write this book, I decided to just write what happened and let the reader do the rest.

According to the Office of Juvenile Justice:

"The first active street gangs in Western Civilization were reported by Pike (1873, pp.276-277) a widely respected chronicler of British crime. He documented the existence of gangs of highway robbers in England during the 17th century, and he speculates that similar gangs might have existed in our mother country much earlier, perhaps as early as the 14th or even the 12th century. But it does not appear that these gangs had the features of modern day, serious street gangs.

"More structured gangs did not appear until the early 1600s, when London was terrorized by a series of organized gangs calling themselves the Mims, Hectors, Bungles, Deadboys...who found amusement in breaking windows, and demolishing taverns and they also fought pitched battles among themselves dressed with colored ribbons to distinguish different factions."[10]

The following is a typed excerpt of a letter Raymond Washington wrote about the Crips in his own words in February of 1978. This was found on Raymond's personal property—after his death—at the apartment where he was living.

The (unedited) letter read: (See Pics 8-9, 8-10)

People that do not really know what they be saying.

People that think and say they really know how the Crips started, but do they really know the real reason on how the Crips started and what do they really know what the Crip started for, and how do they know when the Crip started.

How did they know when the Crips started, Was they a Crip, was they with us when we started the Crips, how do they know are (or) who told them when the Crips started, I wonder sometime.

I know that I didn't tell them about the Crips and when we started Crippin, because who are they to know and tell how we started the Crips, because was they there when we started or was they a Crip.

I know that they didn't go through the thing we went through to start the Crips. They wasn't around when we started so how do they know the really real up on us because we are really wondering why people say anything that they isn't in.

So how do they know the real reason up on us why people lies about the Crips because only ten's of us started the Crips, and some of the brothers that was with us do not even know the real reason because they just wanna to get some help.

Do they really know what we was all about when we frist started and when we frist had that Frist meeting, I do wonder right today what was in they minds when we frist had that meeting togethers.

But do the other's people really know about us, I don't really feel that they don't because all the things I been hearing from them or (are) not "true".

But only what others feel and thing, I just let them thinks it until the real reason and true come out.

Only a few people can tell you the true on how the Crip started and here the true on how we really started and here the reason and why we started the Crip and what we started for and here is some of my reason was for.

What I am really saying or try to say to the people thing that what they really don't know, or can say what they really don't know about, but they still gong be saying things because people always gonna lie about something they do not sincerely know about because what they feel on what others say and they don't really know about it, just be saying thing to starts and say to have something to talk about, because they really do not know about just what others say for what people wants to hear them say but it is just hear.

People put us into all kind of thing, just to get the Crips into something to start between others that do not know better then they know themselfs.

But I know that people wants to say thing about Crips what they really do not know what is Crip all about, because what do they know really about a Crip, what do they really know as what the newspaper say about us and as others say as well too, because the one who say it they just hear other people say a thing just to talk about something so others can go on with the talks about the Crips.

So many say thing to start thing with us to find out so we can be they fool's like they want us to be and they do thing just to put the Crips name on it so the MAN can come to us to take to jail.

I do wonder why people say they they do not know about because if they really knew why we started they would'nt never try to muck to start things.

And that hour reason for starting only Crips from "69" Crips knows how we really started and where we really coming from, and how we see each other.

So people please do not say thing you do not know because you really don't know many thing about us only what you feel about us.

Thank you

"You can get a lot farther with a kind word and a gun
than a kind word alone."

~ Al Capone ~

CHAPTER ONE
RAY'S EARLY LIFE AND FAMILY

"A journey of a thousand miles begins with a single step."
~ Lao Tzu, *The Way of Lao Tzu* ~

Before you can grasp who the man behind the Crips was, you need to understand the environment in which he grew up. The City of Los Angeles, and the violence of the civil rights movement, forged the lens through which Raymond Washington would view the world. Social scientists agree that environment is responsible for most of the choices we make. The rest of our choices are the result of nature, meaning we each have our unique set of gifts, talents, and coping mechanisms. Both nature and nurture would become the anvil that would forge Raymond Washington into a formidable leader, warrior, gang member, tactician, and eventually an urban legend in the punishing and unforgiving streets of Los Angeles.[11]

Raymond Lee Washington was born Friday, August 14, 1953 in Los Angeles, California. (See Pics 8-1, 8-2, 8-3) His mother, Violet Samuel, (See Pic 4-9) gave birth to Raymond, her fourth child, at twenty-three. Raymond was born at 5:45 p.m. at the Los Angeles County General Hospital. Violet, originally a Texas native, was the seventh of nine children. She had moved to California looking for work and lived in Watts at 9221 Firth Boulevard before moving to 850 East 76th Street between Wadsworth and Central Avenue. (See

Pic 6-1) Raymond would grow up in that neighborhood with his three older brothers: Ronald Joe, Donny Ray, and Reggie. (See Pic 4-7) Raymond's parents never married (See Pics 4-1, 4-2) and ended their relationship when Raymond was fairly young. Violet married L.V. Barton on October 17, 1964. They were married for four years and divorced in May of 1968. They had one son together, Violet's last child, Derard Barton. (See Pic 4-10)

When Violet moved into Los Angeles, segregated neighborhoods were very much a fact of life. Black people were severely discouraged from living in the suburbs of the city, restricted instead to living in the mostly black populated neighborhoods in Watts. She would find the environment a difficult one to obtain affordable and safe housing where she could raise her family. Black people moving to Los Angeles in the early 1950s "found themselves excluded from the suburbs and restricted to housing in East or South Los Angeles, which includes the Watts neighborhood, and Compton. Such real estate practices severely restricted educational and economic opportunities available to the minority community. With an influx of black residents, housing in South Los Angeles became increasingly scarce, overwhelming the already established communities. For a time in the early 1950s and with its increasing numbers of African Americans, South Los Angeles became the site of significant racial violence, with whites bombing, firing into, and burning crosses on the lawns of homes purchased by black families south of Slauson Avenue."[12]

Not only were black people segregated into black only neighborhoods, when they arrived in Los Angeles they found what had been a fruitful and bountiful job market during World War II was now disappearing rapidly. There were few—if any—jobs, places to live, and the resources and infrastructures that were present in the previously all white areas of Compton and Watts were now being pulled out and relocated elsewhere in the city. Think of a black only version of *The Grapes of Wrath*, the Pulitzer Prize winning novel by John Steinbeck, and you have a very clear vision of what Violet Samuel and thousands of other black Americans who traveled to Los Angeles from all over the country were facing when they arrived. Except there was one vital difference, *The Grapes of Wrath* was a fictional account of the "Oakies" leaving Oklahoma in search of a better life and finding nothing but despair and poverty. This was a painful reality, and no one wrote a single word about it that did anything meaningful. Los Angeles was a tinderbox waiting to explode. As Steinbeck so masterfully described in *The Grapes of Wrath*, "How can you frighten a man whose hunger is not only in his own cramped stomach but in the wretched bellies of his children? You can't scare him—he has known a fear beyond every other." Unfortunately the lessons of the Great Depression were lost on the civic leaders in Los Angeles in the 50s and 60s. In 1962 John Steinbeck received a Nobel Prize for his writing, meanwhile very real grapes of wrath were growing and festering in the brutal streets of Watts California. Los Angeles was about as explosive and deadly a situation as it could possibly be, and no one in a position to disarm it saw it coming.

The sons of Violet Samuel grew up a lot like all kids do, running through the neighborhood, climbing trees, and jumping fences. They tested themselves against their neighborhood allies by playing street ball in front of their house. They would get up in the morning and walk to the corner of 78th and McKinley to eat breakfast that was being provided by the Black Panther Party at their local chapter house. The Panthers had set up a free breakfast program to provide food for the kids in the area whose parents were unable to do so. The influence of the Panthers would have a huge impact on the mentality of the children as they listened to their "Black Pride" ideology.

Violet's five boys were wild and rambunctious, as most boys are. In an interview with Derard, he started laughing as he recounted a memory he had of being teased by Raymond when they were very young. Raymond was wearing a cast at the time because he had broken his arm on a motorcycle or a mini bike. Their brother, Reggie, had a cast as well; he had cut the tendons on his hand climbing a fence. Derard remembered going to the bathroom where his older brother, Reggie, was taking a bath and complaining about Raymond teasing him. Reggie got out of the tub and told Raymond to "Leave him alone, god damn it!" Raymond took one look at Reggie and punched him with the arm that was in the cast, knocking him back into the tub.

Derard recalled, "Another time Raymond was messing with me and I went and got my BB gun and shot him right in the butt as he was going over the fence. I was little, it was the only way I could defend myself." Another test of boyhood Derard described was standing toe to toe and taking turns punching each other in the chest. "You would stand there and take the hardest punch the other one could give right in the middle chest."

As teenagers, and later grown men, they were all gifted in one way or another. Reggie, the middle child, played in a band and was quite a gifted musician. Three of the brothers would end up serving in the military, both during and after the Vietnam War: Donald Ray and Derard volunteered for the army, and Ronald Joe was drafted in the marines. This was during an era where military service was not seen as the honorable service to your country as it is today. No one came up to you on the street and thanked you for your service as so frequently happens now. People despised the military and frequently spat on military members returning from combat and referred to them as baby killers. The Vietnam War was not popular with the majority of the public. Entering the military was a very quick ticket into a war zone, and made you very unpopular at home, yet all three decided to join. Reggie would enter into a construction company with his fiancées family. This was no family of drug dealers and welfare recipients, they were, and still are, a successful and tight-knit group.

While in Los Angeles doing research for this book, I had the chance to do a brief interview with Raymond's mother and her youngest son, Derard, at her home. She fondly remembered Raymond as a happy boy and a gifted athlete who really "hated going to the dentist." (See Pics 1-1 through 1-5) She remembered leaving for work one day and several police officers coming to arrest her son, not for the first time. She said, "I felt like I was being singled out. As a single parent I was at my wit's end, trying to provide for my family in the inner city and somehow keep them out of trouble while I worked several jobs." She recalled that the police officers told her, "Ma'am, you are not the only one; we are arresting a lot of kids lately." She said it made her feel better knowing that she wasn't alone in the nightmare that was raising a child in South Central Los Angeles, as she watched the police once again drive away with Raymond in their custody.

According to Derard, "When Raymond was in juvenile detention, because he was a fighter, he got noticed right away. If he liked you, you were cool and he would take you under his wing and provide protection. If he liked you, he would protect you. If not, he would beat your ass. It was as simple as that." (See Pic 3-1)

CHAPTER TWO
THE WATTS RIOTS AND RAYMOND'S 12TH BIRTHDAY

"How long? Not long, because 'you shall reap what you sow!'"
~ Martin Luther King, March 25, 1965, Montgomery, Alabama ~

Raymond attended 79th Street Elementary School, (See Pics 2-1, 2-3 through 2-6) and later Edison Junior High and Charles Drew Junior High. As he got older school became more difficult. His education in the streets of Los Angeles didn't fit well with his education in the school system. One was a very real battle for survival while the other promised a better life through education. Raymond could read the writing on the wall. No one he knew had escaped the brutal reality of South Central Los Angeles. It was difficult to believe that there was a life outside of the explosive war zone that Los Angeles was about to become, and it was happening right in front of the twelve-year-old boy's eyes.

The city that Raymond Washington grew up in as a child was one of the most dangerous in the country at the time. The Watts riots would erupt less than a mile from his home the same week as his twelfth birthday. They began when LAPD Motor Officer Lee Minikus arrested Marquette Frye for drunk driving. An article written in the *Los Angeles Times*[13] twenty-five years after the riots gives some insight into what Minikus felt his own culpability in the riots were:

A quarter of a century after the Los Angeles riots, the ex-motorcycle officer says he feels little regret or responsibility for the chaos that visited South Los Angeles that fateful night 25 years ago this month. Although he was saddened by the incident, Minikus said, he has never allowed himself to be cast as "the man who started the Watts riots."

"I was just doing my job," said Minikus, who took early retirement four years ago. "That's why we got paid: to arrest people breaking the law. Marquette was breaking the law."

Minikus said he had not noticed Frye until a man in a pickup truck alerted him to the 1955 Buick Special that Frye was driving.

"I was on my motorcycle, and (the driver) pulled up to me and said, 'See that man? I think he's drunk,'" Minikus recalled. "I noticed Marquette was speeding so I got behind him."

Minikus said he followed the Buick up El Segundo Boulevard and stopped Frye at 116th Place and Avalon Boulevard. When he walked over to the car, Minikus said he noticed immediately that Frye appeared drunk.

When Frye climbed out of the automobile, Minikus said, the officer put him through a series of sobriety tests that Frye failed.

"I told him he was under arrest, but he was real nice about it," Minikus said. "He was joking around, putting on a show for the crowd that had started to gather. I was even laughing."

Minikus said the laughter swiftly turned to rage when Frye's mother, Rena, showed up. She scolded her son for being drunk, Minikus said, and suddenly Marquette became surly.

When Minikus tried to arrest Frye, he jumped back and verbally snapped at the officer for the first time. Minikus' partner, Bob Lewis, who had shown up as the crowd grew, called for backup officers.

"It might have been easier to have dropped it right there, but it's hard to back away at that point," Minikus said. "I had already told the guy he was under arrest."

Minikus said that, when the backup officers started arriving minutes later, one of them tried to stop Frye from disappearing into the crowd.

A backup officer tried to hit Marquette on the arm with a ba-
ton, Minikus said. "But Marquette bent over and was hit just
above the eye."

Frye backed into Minikus, who grabbed him to place him in one
of the patrol cars. Then Frye's brother punched Minikus in the kid-
ney, the officer recalled, and their mother jumped on his back and
tore his shirt.

"We put them all in the same car, and then the officers began
leaving the scene," Minikus said. "But the crowd had gotten really
angry by this time. I didn't stay around to see what happened."

The riots ensued. After an officer tried to arrest a woman he be-
lieved had spit on him during the Frye arrests, the crowd grew more
enraged by what they believed was his abuse of the woman. They
tossed bottles at the patrol car as the backup officers sped away, the
woman in the back seat.

Officer Minikus claimed to have been unaware of the effect the arrest had on the public until much later. This wasn't surprising. In my experience, it was the typical mentality of a traffic cop. They saw the world as black and white, right and wrong. There were no shades of gray in their mind. The "I was just doing my job" was a very narrow focus on the real issues that a cop experienced on a daily basis. It could be extremely comforting for the officer to see his own actions and not the bigger picture. This made him a part of the problem, via apathy, rather than becoming part of the solution. The results were obvious, and even after this riot and the obvious message it sent, they again became obvious in 1992, after the verdict in the Rodney King trial, and the following riots. Nothing had changed.

It was likely that Raymond Washington had no idea at the time what had started the Watts riots. Realistically, he probably didn't care. The reality, though, was that the city he lived in was instantly transformed into a very real war zone.[14] Within a few hours of the original traffic stop, the city was engulfed in rioting. Residents in the area were attacking any police officer they found by shooting guns, and throwing bricks, rocks and chunks of concrete at their cars as they responded into affected areas. Buildings were burning and snipers were on the rooftops shooting at police.[15] On the second day of the rioting, Raymond woke to a city transformed. The Police

Chief, William H. Parker, requested the assistance of the National Guard to stop the rioting because the LAPD had lost control of the forty-six square mile swath of the city affected by it. Raymond would have witnessed armed national guardsmen carrying rifles, and walking on foot patrols similar to the patrols carried out in the jungles of Vietnam. Soldiers with bayonets attached to their rifles walked the streets.[16]

Any normal child would have seen this chaos and open warfare in the street and most likely been too afraid to leave the presumed safety of their homes. Raymond Washington was not a normal kid. Fearless, self-confident, and defiant, he didn't understand—or didn't care—about the danger that surrounded him as he left the house on the night of his twelfth birthday, during the peak of the riots. Raymond's younger brother, Derard, said, "Raymond snuck out of the house late one night during the riots. I thought he was crazy but there was no stopping him." Derard told me that Raymond snuck around cautiously, avoiding the several thousand national guardsmen, and nearly two thousand police officers in the area. Not to mention the snipers and looters. Gunfire and screams were heard throughout the night as "Raymond made his way to a nearby White Front sporting goods store[17] that had been being looted. He returned home a while later, dragging a huge box of basketballs, footballs, softballs, and sporting goods he had taken from the damaged store." (See Pic 2-7)

I had to laugh as Derard shared this story. I imagined the twelve-year-old boy dragging a huge box of sporting goods equipment three-quarters of a mile from the store to his home, skillfully avoiding the police and armed adults, as they battled in the area. I imagined him coming into his mother's home with a huge smile on his face, covered in sweat, victorious in his nighttime covert raid, his twelfth birthday a memorable one.

This account gave me a lot of insight into the man who would emerge from the young boy, someone already skilled at moving stealthily and able to conduct successful "tactical operations" in an urban environment at twelve-years-old. Ray had conducted what the military would refer to as an "incursion"—defined as "a hostile entrance into or invasion of a place or territory, especially a sudden one."[18]

He had done it in the dead of night against an occupational force and succeeded (just like his heroes in the war movies). I pointed that out to

Derard, and he said, "Yes, Raymond loved watching war movies, over and over again. He also loved watching the old gangster movies that had the 1930 era gangsters portrayed by James Cagney and Edward G. Robinson. He was obsessed with them and wanted to learn everything about them, trying to be like them." The lessons that those movies taught were obvious and based much more in the reality Raymond lived with in Los Angeles. You succeeded by being tougher, smarter, stronger, more prepared and, if need be, more brutal than your enemies. This made a lot more sense to his sixth-grade mind than the lessons being taught by his teachers in elementary school. (See Pic 2-6)

Derard also remarked, "Raymond also loved to play with those little plastic army guys we had as kids. But for him it was an obsession. He used real tactics and carefully planned his mini war games with an attention to detail I could never understand." Derard said that Raymond continued to play with the toys into his teens. To the uninitiated that would appear harmless, however, those same exercises conducted by twelve-year-old boys all over America are now referred to as "tabletop exercises," and are frequently used by the military today to visually prepare battlefield commanders. It is thought to give them a mental frame of reference for how the battlefield should look. They are also used by emergency service response teams all over the world to prepare for natural and man-made disasters such as earthquakes or terrorist attacks, and are seen as an extremely valuable training tool. Raymond Washington was in battlefield training at twelve-years-old. He would later be referred to as the "Brigadier General of South Los Angeles" by *Allhood Publications* (2008).

Perhaps you would think, as I did, that Raymond kept the huge box of basketballs, footballs, softballs, and baseballs to himself. He had braved the dangers of the Watts riots, snipers on the rooftops, armed looters, and national guardsmen armed with bayonet-tipped rifles patrolling the city. The use of the bayonet against American citizens rather than against enemy combatants in a war zone shows the extreme measures being taken during the Watts riots. The bayonet is a dagger-like steel weapon that is attached to or at the muzzle of a gun and used for stabbing or slashing in hand-to-hand combat. Formerly it had only been used by the army in warfare against enemy combatants in a war zone.[19] It was now being employed against American citizens. I would have kept the equipment, but Raymond did not. According to Derard, "He gave them all to the neighborhood kids." Already, Raymond was forging alliances, leveraging relationships with his peers, and showing his future leadership style. Granted, it was with stolen property, but the legend that Raymond Washington would become was being born. He did Robin Hood like charity on one hand, and on the other, he conducted fearless raids into enemy territory against overwhelming odds, and lived for battle in the streets of Los Angeles.

Ray Rhone remembers the Watts riots as well. As Raymond Washington's cousin, he had spent a lot of time with him growing up. When I asked about the Watts riots and the White Front store, I expected him to recall the same story as Derard. Instead, he recalled watching Billy "Big Law" Ray and Bobby "Lil Law" Ray kick in the front windows of the White Front store as people waited to loot it.[20] Rhone recalled Big Law and Lil Law were legends on Slauson Avenue. "They were much older than us but they had larger than life reputations in the area."

When the Watts riots were over, fourteen thousand national guardsmen had flooded the area, along with nine hundred thirty-four officers from the LAPD, and seven hundred eighteen deputies from LASD. Approximately thirty-five thousand adults (Los Angeles citizens) participated in the riots by battling with police. Over the course of six days, nearly one thousand buildings were burned or damaged, one hundred ninety-two businesses were looted, and forty million dollars in damage was caused. Additionally thirty-four people were killed, one thousand thirty-two were injured, and three thousand four hundred thirty-eight were arrested. Ninety police officers were also injured.[21]

Raymond Washington had a front row seat to everything that happened that week. I believe given his natural abilities, determination and with no other venue to channel his drive, he was well on his way to making the decisions that would enable him to take control of the city's gang culture, and the timing of the Watts riots helped to make that a reality. The breakdown of social order and the reality of just how thin the veil of security everyone naively comes to accept as a steadfast reality could not have been lost on Raymond. He had ventured out into the night and witnessed firsthand the brutal beatings and open-armed combat that his neighbors were having with the accepted leaders and enforcers of our society. How could that not have deeply affected him?

The Watts riots were not the only events of the era that most likely framed Raymond's view of the world. Looking back through the events of the time, there were several notable incidents that caused many to question just how fairly they were being treated by the government, and how trustworthy authority figures within the society really were.

John "Moon" McDaniels, an original member of the Crips, recalled the first time he met Raymond Washington. I interviewed McDaniels as he, Derard Barton, and I sat in a car behind Fremont High School in an incredibly hard rainstorm in the early spring of 2014. Derard and John had not seen each other in over thirty years, and it took some work on Derard's part to locate McDaniels and convince him to meet with us. He is one of the few surviving members of the original Crips, and was a close friend of Raymond Washington. He still very much identifies with his status as an original member of the Crips, and continues to carry himself with the confidence and swagger of someone who survived many gang battles on the street.

He told me the story of meeting Raymond and John Clough as he entered his homeroom at Edison Junior High School. As McDaniels entered the classroom, he found Raymond and Clough in a playful but heated battle, throwing the felt erasers from the chalkboards at each other from opposite ends of the room. He watched the battle for a moment and then convinced them to stop before they were caught and punished by the teacher. Surprisingly, they both did stop and this was the beginning of a friendship that would last until they were separated by death. According to McDaniels, he and Craig Craddock were some of the select few who could reign Raymond in and make him think about the consequences before he took a particular course of action.

Speaking to me more than thirty-five years after the death of Raymond Washington, tears filled McDaniels' eyes as he talked about Raymond and Craig Craddock. He said, "All that bullshit you have heard about all these other people claiming to be founders or co-founders of the Crips is lies, fucking lies told by people that would never have dared to speak up if Raymond and Craig were still alive. Tookie Williams was no co-founder, and neither was Greg 'Batman' Davis. All those people out there like Mike Concepcion, and whoever else, they were members, true, we all were, but there was only two at the beginning, only two! Raymond Washington and Craig Craddock. Period. Anything anyone else tells you is an outright lie, make sure that you put that in the book!"

Marcus Jones, another associate of Raymond, also agreed to be interviewed. He began by telling me the story of how he met Raymond and formed a friendship that lasted until Raymond's death. He recalls that he was, "Maybe ten years old and playing in the construction site for the White Front store that was being rebuilt after the first Watts riots in 1965. The store had been burned out and looted during the riots, and they were rebuilding it. The area in Compton and Watts was filled with blacks from all over the country and they had banded together and stayed in tight groups based on where they were from. A group of bullies came at me and a kid I knew as Lil Tookie and they tried to beat us up and rob us taking our toys and whatever else we had that they wanted. (See Pic 2-2) I was standing up for Lil Tookie and then here came Raymond. He was already a fighter, and he helped us battle with the older stronger bullies." From that day on, Jones said, he and Raymond were friends. He described Raymond as a protector, a fearless fighter, and a mentor. Surprisingly, though, he said that Raymond himself could be a bully at times, and recalled that Raymond would wait out front of that very same store and rob other kids of their money. Jones said that Raymond never robbed him, and they always got along very well, but that the kids Raymond did not like did not fare so well.

While I was interviewing John McDaniels and Derard Barton, I asked a lot of random questions to try and spark their memories of minor details that might help me to see the whole picture of who Raymond was at a younger age. I asked what his favorite color was. Neither knew the answer—although I admit, for obvious reasons, I assumed it would be blue. I asked about his favorite food, neither man knew. When I asked, however, what his favorite songs were, the duo erupted into song. I must admit that I was speechless. Here I was on the side of the road in South Central Los Angeles, sitting behind Fremont High School near the visiting teams bleachers with two older members of the Crips, both of whom had survived many gang battles—each having been shot at least once—and they began to sing. They got into a heated argument over which song was actually Raymond's favorite, yelling from the front seat to the back. Finally they reached an agreement, Raymond liked different songs at different times in his childhood, and they listed them off as they took turns at cranking out the melodies. The first song they mentioned was "I Only Meant To Wet My Feet" by The Whispers, 1972.[22] The second song was again by The Whispers and was titled "Seems Like I Gotta Do Wrong," 1970.[23] The third that they recalled was by the Temptations and titled "Run Away Child, Running Wild," 1969.[24] Finally, they both agreed that as Raymond grew older he liked the song, "It's The Way Nature Planned It" by The Four Tops, 1972.[25]

Listening to the songs, I discovered two distinct themes. Two were love songs, which honestly surprised me, and two were songs about feeling alone, and struggling with daily life in the inner city. I think the music said a lot about the duality and inner turmoil found in Raymond Washington's behavior and actions as they were recalled by his friends and family.

Ray Rhone recalled that when he and Raymond were younger, they were both watched by Raymond's grandmother. Violet and L.V. Barton had day jobs, so Raymond's grandmother was left in charge of them. When they got into trouble, their grandmother used corporal punishment, whipping them to make her point. Rhone said he vividly remembered that no matter how hard she punished Raymond, he refused to cry. Raymond just stared at her, showing no emotion. This refusal to subordinate to his grandmother's punishment would establish a pattern in Raymond's life that would be noted by nearly everyone who knew him. He would never give an inch in the face of adversity. He was very capable of negotiation when he did not feel backed into a corner, however, he would never be threatened or forced into doing anything by anyone. (See Pics 2-1, 2-3)

Speaking about growing up in South Central Los Angeles, Derard said, "Everyone in the neighborhood had a nickname, and they banded together in small groups to protect each other against rival neighborhoods." This is normal behavior for any neighborhood children: grouping together for protection from your enemies. Derard said that Raymond's only known nickname was simply "Ray Ray." Later, as he entered the city's gang culture, transforming the streets with his notorious Crips, he would never be known by any name other than Raymond Washington. According to Derard, "Raymond did not need a nickname. His was a reputation that required nothing but his real name for people to know and understand who he was. Everyone knew who Raymond Washington was."

Raymond's older brother, Reggie, was extremely bowlegged and had a very distinct and unusual gait. Derard laughed as he recalled that, "Reggie was a talented musician. He played in the Fremont High School band and the Florence youth band. All of his friends had nicknames and had them sewn into their shirts and wrote them on their shoes with Bleach and Q-tips. The band members included had given him the nickname "Crip," you know how kids can be? So we called him Crip too because he walked so funny. He was proud of the name and wrote it on his shoes and embroidered it in his shirts. He was constantly teased about being Crip." (See Pics 4-3, 4-5)

After Derard's parents divorced, the older boys took on a lot more of the parenting and protective role their father had held while their mother worked several jobs. Raymond's brother, Ronald, recalled that they would go to a community swimming pool at Roosevelt Park during the summer. "Raymond and his friends would meet up and walk to the park at 76th and Graham in the unincorporated Florence area of South Central Los Angeles. Raymond loved to do backward midair somersaults off of the diving board. Raymond swam there often and was befriended by the lifeguard Robert E. Mosley." (*Allhood Publications*, 2008). Mosley would teach Raymond how to tumble, and some basic gymnastics. Raymond was already an exceptional athlete. Mosley became one of many famous mentors in Raymond's life. He would later become famous for his role in the *Magnum, P.I.* television series for his portrayal of the helicopter pilot Theodore "TC" Calvin.[26]

Raphael Pattaway grew up in the same neighborhood as Raymond Washington, and had this to say about it, "One big part of our all growing up together was the Savoy Skating Rink on Central Avenue and 77th Street. Raymond's first gang he was in was called the Avenues and we all used to go to the Savoy Skating Rink. A lot of reputations were established there, a lot of fights came out of there. People would skate and stuff and then after there would be fights, and Raymond would always win. Always!" I asked Raphy why he thought Raymond always won the fights. He laughed and said, "Raymond was always very athletic and built. He had amazing physical capabilities. He had a very competitive mentality and refused to lose at everything he did. He had to be the best at anything he did. He put his all into it. When I was little I had a bicycle. Raymond was always asking if he could borrow my bicycle. He got me on that a few times. He would borrow it and be gone all day. He said that he was just going to the store but he would be gone for five or six hours. He always brought the bike back though, he never stole it. You loaned him your bike and you knew it was gonna be gone all day! He was a good cat. I knew him and grew up with him; I have known him all my life."

Marcus Jones also recalled Raymond as being very athletic and very good at gymnastics. He said, "As kids we used to get together and do flips off of inner tubes from car tires. We would jump on them and then try to do back flips, front flips and land on our feet. I was not as good at it as Raymond. He could do some amazing gymnastic feats!" (See Pic 3-2)

Raymond eventually became more and more detached from the school system. He would be thrown out of nearly every school in the Los Angeles unified school district and then shipped out to the county schools. He was an accomplished fighter, and upon entering a new school, he would challenge the tougher and larger kids to fights to establish himself as someone not to be messed with. This habit would solidify his reputation early among the kids in the inner-city schools. The last school he attended was Fremont High School. Years later, when the reputation of Raymond Washington as the founder and leader of the Crips was solidly established, kids who had witnessed Raymond's schoolyard battles would remember him and the ferocity of those battles. The legend of Raymond Washington had already begun to form and was only magnified as he became known as the founder of the Crips.

Jones recalled that even before Raymond had founded the Crips, "He would tell me to go with him when he went into other neighborhoods. We never did this, the neighborhoods were clannish and the different people from different parts of the country stuck together. It was dangerous to go into a strange neighborhood, but Raymond had this personality, he knew all the mommas and sisters of everyone in the different areas, so we were cool. Even then he was known as Raymond Washington. He was welcome in neighborhoods where others were not. I would not have dared to go into the neighborhoods he took me but when people saw me with him, I was accepted immediately. We would walk through Watts, Compton and everyone knew Raymond." Even with the formation of the Crips a few years away, Raymond had already established the social skills, contacts, and relationships that would enable him to unite the neighborhoods of South Central Los Angeles under the blue flag of the Crips.

At about this time, urban leaders were under attack. Malcolm X was a notable leader who had made the transition from street thug to national figure. He originally preached a doctrine of rebellion and open confrontation with the established order and power structure of the United States. However, after a pilgrimage to Mecca in 1964, he too had an epiphany and realized we are all in this battle together. *MalcolmX.com* described the pilgrimage in this way, "Malcolm went on a pilgrimage to Mecca, which proved to be life altering for him. For the first time, Malcolm shared his thoughts and beliefs with different cultures and found the response to be overwhelmingly positive. When he returned, Malcolm said he had met 'blond-haired, blued-eyed men I could call my brothers.' He returned to the United States with a new outlook on integration and a new hope for the future. This time when Malcolm spoke, instead of just preaching to African-Americans, he had a message for all races.[27] Malcolm X was assassinated by Thomas Hagen and two others in 1965.[28]

Alprentice "Bunchy" Carter was another local leader that Raymond most likely would have known and looked up to. He was a member of the Slauson Street gang in Los Angeles and earned the nickname "the Mayor of the Ghetto" for his toughness and criminal activities. He served time in prison and was influenced by the teachings of Islam and of Malcolm X. After his release from prison, Carter met Huey Newton, and joined the Black Panther Party. He went on to form the Southern Californian chapter of the Black Panthers, and became a leader in the group. They read political literature, trained in firearms and first aid, and began a "free breakfast for children" program to feed impoverished children in the area.[29] According to Derard, "Raymond and my brothers would attend the free breakfast program every morning, going over to get breakfast and hearing the words that the Black Panthers had spread." The FBI had a secret operation that investigated the Black Panthers, and J. Edgar Hoover considered them, "the greatest threat to the internal security of the country." The FBI worked with the LAPD to intimidate and harass the party members. The Black Panthers were under constant surveillance and had been infiltrated by the FBI.

I know my mindset as a cop was that if they were not doing anything wrong, the police would have left them alone. This was not the feeling of the people in the communities of South Central Los Angeles. Later, I would realize that their suspicions were founded in their reality, which was so very different to my own. The Panthers were seen as heroes, who stood up for their communities, using whatever means necessary to break the death grip they felt the government and/or the establishment had on the black community.

Surprisingly, black nationalist organizations in Los Angeles were at war with each other while trying to unify the black population. The Black Panthers were in a tense standoff with the "US Organization." Later it was revealed that the FBI had intended to mail a letter to the Black Panther Party. A fabricated letter detailing plans to ambush their members. The FBI was employing psychological warfare tactics on the two groups, attempting to get them to turn on each other. Bunchy Carter and fellow Panther John Huggins were killed in an argument with the "US Organization" in a meeting in 1969 at UCLA.[30]

Bunchy Carter grew up in Los Angeles. He was well known in the streets, and no doubt known to Raymond Washington as they lived in the same neighborhood. The ideas that he represented and the manner in which he died could not have been lost on Raymond. James Ward grew up with Raymond Washington and along with Marcus Jones would later describe to me the effect that Carter and the Black Panthers had on the Crips. James Ward said, "The Black Panther influence was one very significant factor that separated the East side Crips from the West side Crips. The East side had a militant mentality which came from their association with the Black Panthers as children. Seeing the Panthers shoot it out with the cops, and the nation of Islam going around recruiting members had effect on us and that the East side was all about bringing up the black people and culture while the West side had no such influence and it showed in the way they carried themselves and how they perceived what the Crips were all about." Marcus said a lot of the incidents that the Crips were blamed for actually came from things the West side Crips had done and their lack of understanding of what the Crips were supposed to be about. Alleged gang experts claim the Black Panther influence on the original militant ideology of the Crips is a stretch at best. One article remarked that there was no proven origin of the name Crips, and that most likely it "originated from the ditty bop strut of gang members as if they were crippled." Additionally the article stated that the "Crips were thugs that preyed on their community and other blacks and that Black Panthers would have been strongly against that."[31]

Already a trend was being established of "black on black" violence. Additionally, it had to be obvious to Raymond that he could trust no one but his inner circle, anyone could be corrupted against him if the right motivation was found. Trusting someone who was assumed to be an ally was something that later cost Raymond his life.

As a cop working in the Western United States I could not understand the suspicion the black community had of the police. It seemed out of place with the times. I, however, had not been raised with these stories, and I was not immersed in this culture like Raymond had been. I do recall one day having a rather disturbing epiphany as I watched the evening news.

Geronimo Pratt was a Black Panther leader who had been released from prison. He had been under surveillance by the FBI when Caroline Olsen, a schoolteacher, was kidnapped and murdered. Pratt maintained that he could not have done the murder as he was at a Black Panther meeting the day of the murder. He was telling the truth and the FBI knew it. Instead of freeing him, they destroyed the surveillance tapes, which would have proven his innocence. Pratt served twenty-seven years for an abduction and murder he did not commit. There were people who had been at the Black Panther meeting who could testify that Pratt had attended, but their voices were never heard.[32]

I could imagine how that would severely affect people's trust of the government. I know it rocked my own confidence in the system, even though I was already a part of it. From that point on, I too was extremely skeptical. Pratt was targeted, and convicted of a murder he did not commit, and evidence that proved he could not have possibly committed the crime was suppressed by the very agencies that were supposed to protect us all. I am sure this story spread like wildfire through the black community. The outrage must have been intense. I don't think there was anyway that Raymond would not have caught wind of it, and the implications as to the intentions of the police at the time.

All of these events occurred as Raymond Washington grew up in South Central Los Angeles. The lessons were clear: nothing was fair. Right and wrong were clearly warped and disfigured by the powers that be and the only way to not be subjected to the abuse of an authority figure was to become an authority figure. Raymond Washington set out looking for a way to do exactly that.

Kumasi Washington of Slauson Street explained the events after the slaughter of urban leaders in the 1960s in this way: "They ran them down, they chased them down, they hunted them down, they murdered everybody they could and made everybody else either go into exile, or they locked them up in the penitentiary. And when all that was over with a new element rose up called the *Crips*, ya see? And then the shit started again."[33]

CHAPTER THREE
THE AVENUES

According to popular myth, the Avenue Boys gang was one of the more prominent and violent gangs in South Central Los Angeles (not to be confused with the Avenues or "Avenidas" a Sureños set that had and still has a deep and well-known hatred of black people). The gang was being led by an athletic and muscular teen: Craig Munson. Raymond joined the gang in his early teens and reportedly had an altercation with Craig's younger brother. Craig did not appreciate his younger brother being beaten up by Raymond, so he retaliated. [6]

Another account of Raymond's split from the Avenue Boys is in *All-hood Publications* (2008). It says, "Raymond's oldest brother and Craig Munson got into a fight, shortly after Raymond got into a fight with Big Pookie (East side Pookie) after slapping Pookie with an open fist. Pookie was one of Munson's protégés and was given the name Baby Munson. Big Munson and Baby Munson got together and retaliated against Raymond and disciplined him." This allegedly resulted in the split of Raymond Washington from the Avenue Boys. According to the article, this was in 1969 and Raymond was attending Edison Junior High School. The article goes on to say that he went there and organized a group of neighborhood friends, and founded the Baby Cribs in admiration for the Avenue Boys. The article explains that the name "cribs" was relative to the younger generation and used to mean babies or the younger generation of a gang. So in effect it meant the Baby Avenues.

Analyzing this critically, with my knowledge of gangs and gang membership, it makes absolutely no sense. I have never witnessed a falling out like Raymond Washington is alleged to have had with Craig Munson and Baby Munson, where the exiled gang member then went on to form their own gang out of admiration for the one they'd been exiled from. Perhaps to the layperson this makes sense, I cannot accept it as factual. This account of why Raymond left the Avenue Boys is widely and blindly accepted as truth and fact. Why would Raymond pay homage to the gang he just left on such bad terms? If anything I would expect the exact opposite to be the case.

The more I investigated the specific details of Raymond Washington's life, and specifically anything surrounding the formation of the Crips, the less I found facts and the more I found fiction, a whole hell of a lot of fiction. Like I said before the myth that surrounded Raymond Washington grew, and continues to grow, as facts become blurred and original witnesses to the events die off. Here are some of the more creative accounts of the formation of the Crips.

According to *A Guide to Understanding Street Gangs* by Al Valdez intended for law enforcement use only, "One of the most popular perspectives presented to law enforcement has been called the Washington High School history. By the 1970s the most popular gang in Watts California was a gang called the Avenue Boys. The gang was led by Craig Munson, Stanley 'Tookie' Williams and Raymond Washington. They developed a unique style of dress that was just as intimidating as their reputations. The Avenue Boys wore Al Capone style hats, leather coats, and Levi's or sharkskin pants. They also wore an earring in the left ear, and used walking sticks or closed umbrellas when they walked."

The story continues, "Raymond separated from the Avenue Boys and moved to West Los Angeles, where he attended Washington High School. Raymond developed a new following and gang members wore distinctive clothing that separated them from other street gangs. His new gang used blue handkerchiefs, blue sweatshirts and Levi's blue jeans, tennis shoes and baseball caps. Additionally Raymond is reported to always walk with a cane. Raymond, Tookie Williams, and another guy named Michael Concepcion began to victimize students that attended Centennial High School. They would steal leather sleeved varsity jackets and in a short period of time they developed a significant following."

According to the story, "Sylvester Scott and Benson Owens were attacked by Stanley 'Tookie' Williams and Raymond Washington along with a small group of followers." Here is where it gets really imaginative: "Washington was reported to have been confined to a wheelchair after being severely injured in a gang related incident. Benson and Scott refused to be intimidated and victimized and fought off their attackers. They claimed to have lived on Piru Street in Compton. As the fight ended the two groups exchanged words and allegedly someone in Benson's group made the comment as the wheelchair bound Raymond Washington and Stanley 'Tookie' Williams were leaving 'don't mess with anyone from Piru Street and take that Crip nigger with you.'"

Scott later claimed to be the founder of the first Blood set, Piru Street, and Benson claims to have founded the West side Pirus.

This is an imaginative but severely flawed account of the split Raymond had with the Avenue Boys, and the reason for the name "Crips." Raymond never lived on the West side of Los Angeles, and he was never confined to a wheelchair for any reason. Al Valdez, the author of the book, had obviously been duped by the Bloods gang members he had interviewed.

Perhaps the reason for the wheelchair myth can be answered by looking at another former gang member, and now musical producer, Mike "Shaft" Concepcion. He appeared on the BET TV channel and made the claim that he was a founder of the Crips. Concepcion appeared with actor James Amos on The Mo'Nique Show. They were there to promote an anti-gang program they had designed called Gangs at Sea. They claimed that removing the gang members from Central Los Angeles to an isolated island at sea for three days would end their hatred for each other. They made the ridiculous claim that the gang members went from bitter enemies to singing songs by a campfire in just three days.[34] Perhaps this is where the idea that Raymond Washington had been confined to a wheelchair came from, and that is where this particular myth about the name of the gang originated.

I asked Derard if he knew what the real reason was for the split between Raymond and the Avenue Boys. He laughed, and said, "Yeah, you have to understand my brother, Reggie, was a talented musician. He played in the Fremont High School band and the Florence youth band—playing the flute and piccolo—and he was also very popular at school. In 1969, Reggie was voted the homecoming king at the high school he attended. Craig Munson's girlfriend had been voted the homecoming queen, and Munson felt that Reggie was paying far too much attention to his girlfriend since they were the king and queen of the dance. After the homecoming dance was over, Craig Munson was jealous of Reggie and pissed off.

"So Craig confronted Reggie, and he pulled a gun on my brother, sticking the gun in his face telling him to step off of his girl. Reggie was pretty shook up, you know? When my big brother, Ronald Joe, found out about the incident he went looking for Munson. He found him at 81st and Avalon. Munson was there at a hamburger joint hanging out and Ronald Joe 'put in some work' on Munson. He made sure that Munson knew that he made a serious mistake pulling a gun on Reggie. Raymond went looking for the younger Munson to make his point as well." Derard said he did not know what happened, but heard that Craig Munson might have tried to punish Raymond for the fight. Derard said he remembered, "Seeing Raymond with a busted lip at that time, and I think that the fight with Munson may have been the reason."

Whether or not Raymond left the Avenues because of the incident between Reggie and Craig, or if he left because of a fight with Craig and Baby Munson, he did leave the Avenues saying, "Fuck the Avenues! I am gonna start my own gang."

I found this to be a much more credible account of the split. It makes more sense than a story where Raymond leaves the gang after being beaten up, and yet is brimming with admiration for the people who had just kicked his ass. As a side note: this account of Raymond leaving the Avenues gang and then forming his own gang, and naming it out of respect and admiration for them is the first and the only account I have ever found in all my research of Raymond Washington ever losing a fight.

If there was a pivotal moment that could have derailed the formation of the Crips, perhaps this one incident is it. If the incident with the Avenues had played out differently, who knows what would have happened. I don't know, but I can see that this was the place in Raymond's life that if he had taken a left turn instead of a right, a lot of his enemies might have survived. Literally thousands of lives would most likely have been saved had things gone differently. In the documentary, *Crips and Bloods: Made in America*, narrated by Forest Whitaker, a gang detective makes the claim that there were fifteen thousand known gang-related deaths at the time of filming.[33] It would not be wise in a few short months from this split with the Avenues to be an enemy of Raymond Lee Washington.

The account Derard Barton gave of Raymond Washington splitting from the Avenue Boys is certainly more accurate than many of the stories being passed around, but it still does not answer the question: where did the name of the gang came from?

While doing research in books and articles written by academics, people in law enforcement, and "retired" or former Crips gang members, I found there to be many stories about where the name for the gang originated.

The book *A Guide to Understanding Street Gangs* (1998), lists three additional and different accounts on how the Crips got their name:

- The first was that Raymond Washington always used a cane when he walked and had been rumored to have needed a wheelchair at some point. The theory goes that crip was short for cripple, and was applied to his gang and that explained the birth of the Crips.
- The second, and perhaps most outrageous theory, is that the name of the Crips came from the HBO series *Tales From the Crypt*.
- The third theory in the book is that the Crips gang is really an offshoot from the Slauson Street gang known as the Cribs. This same account lists the Crips as rivals to the Slauson Street gang, and that they were engaged in gang fights from 1962-1965. Raymond would have been between nine and twelve-years-old at that time, and it would be four years before Raymond would form the Crips.

Recent gang intelligence received from law enforcement at the time the book was written was that "the gang wanted the name of the set to represent the toughest men imaginable. They came up with the name 'Superman.' The only thing that can hurt Superman is Kryptonite, and the theory goes that the phonetically spoken and abbreviated term Crip was developed."

The Crips moniker is variously attributed to the way members walked with a shuffle like a limp, to the sporting of canes or to a mispronunciation of Crib Avenues or Cribs, a term for younger gangsters.[35]

The website *Gangpreventionservices.org* claims "There are many different versions of how the name came to be about and none of them are documented for sure. The most likely reason for the gang's name was the way they walked which was a ditty-bop strut as if crippled. Some people will state that founder Washington carried around a picture of a baby crib, but decided to call the gang Crips."[31]

As a former gang cop I found out very early that law enforcement is usually the last place you should go to find out the truth of what is going on in a gang. Ask cops the reason for a particular gang's name or why they are doing what they are doing, and you will get a lot of theories, not a lot of facts. If you want facts, go straight to the gang and ask. Simple as that. In the city I worked in we had a very dominating Crips gang that was led by a charismatic and dynamic leader very similar to Raymond Washington. The gang's name was OVG. The meaning behind the name was always clouded in mystery for the people outside of the set. We guessed that the name referred to the geographical location of the founder. He lived in the west end of the city, and the area could only be reached by going over a raised viaduct, which connected the West side of the city to the east, while spanning the rail yards. It was thought that OVG stood for Over the Viaduct Gang. Another theory was that the acronym stood for the Original Violent Gangsters. Years later I asked a senior member of the set what the meaning behind the name was. He replied, "It was simple really, Ogden's Violent Gangsters. Simple." He said, "We used to laugh at all the bullshit that the cops came up with trying to explain what our name was, what it meant. They could never get it right!" [36]

I asked Derard where Raymond came up with the name. Derard laughed, and said, "No matter what you read and no matter what others who are in the gang or in the neighborhood have told you, no one knows where Raymond came up with the name except family members, and only immediate family members! The rest is just speculation, hearsay, and wrong."

The rules of evidence in a court of law say that hearsay is not admissible as evidence. It is considered so unreliable that it takes a remarkable set of circumstances for the judge to even consider it. Hearsay evidence is defined as "evidence based not on a witness's personal knowledge but on another's statement not made under oath."[37]

Witness testimony is defined as "testimony made by a person who makes a statement in a court about what he or she knows or has seen or a person who makes a statement in a court about what he or she knows or has actually seen."[38]

Derard's point was to question how anyone could believe all the hearsay out there, rather than questioning the people who were actually there when it all started. The people who had actually witnessed the events. He said, "There were three people there when Raymond was trying to decide what to name the gang, two are dead now, that would be my brother, Raymond, and his best friend, Craig Craddock. If anyone was a co-founder in the gang it would have been Craig Craddock. Others have claimed to have been co-founders or founding members but that is an exaggeration. They were not there when the gang was formed. I was."

Derard was a witness to the conversation between Raymond and Craig Craddock as they tossed ideas back and forth about what to name the gang, what colors to wear, how to refer to the member's different designated ages and genders. He watched as the entire gang's internal structure and culture was laid out by his big brother, Raymond, and Craig Craddock.

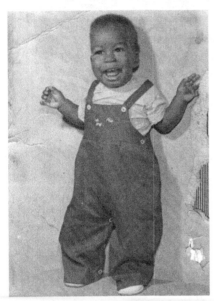 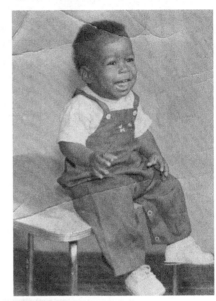

Pic 1-1 (left), Pic 1-2 (right), Pic 1-3 (below):
Raymond at age 18 months

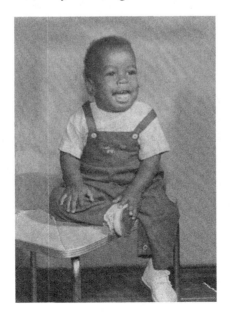

Pic 1-4: Raymond at age 18 months

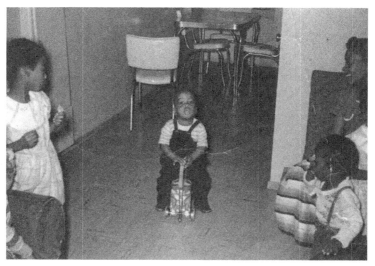

Pic 1-5: Raymond riding a scooter at age 18 months

Pic 2-1: Raymond in 3rd grade

Pic 2-2: Raymond standing between two L.A. Dodgers baseball players
Tommy H. Davis and Willie H. Davis making an appearance
at the White Front store (before the Watts riot)

Pic 2-3: Raymond, age 10, sitting on his bike. Derard (right) standing and smiling

SEVENTY-NINTH STREET SCHOOL
LOS ANGELES
APRIL 1965

MRS. STARKS   GRADE 5

*Pic 2-4: 5ᵗʰ grade class photo: Raymond (top row, eighth from the left)
and Craig Craddock (second row, fifth from the left)*

Pic 2-5: Raymond in 5th grade

*Pic 2-6: Raymond
graduating elementary school*

Pic 2-7: Raymond and Derard

*Pic 3-1: Raymond,
Derard Barton (14), and
Violet Samuel
at Juvenile lockup*

*Pic 3-2: Raymond Washington
(right) flexing at 16*

Pic 3-4: Raymond at the Watts Festival, 1971

Pic 3-4: Raymond center, Peewee (right, in white shirt), and Craig Craddock's girlfriend, Clairette (left, in brown jacket)

Pic 3-5: Raymond(kneeling) with his girlfriend, Peewee (right).
She is the Mother of his only son, Lil Ray

Pic 3-6: Raymond and girlfriend, Peewee

CHAPTER FOUR
FORMING THE CRIPS

"Take things as they are. Punch when you have to punch.
Kick when you have to kick."
~ Bruce Lee ~

The *Learners Dictionary* defines a "founder" as "a person who creates or establishes something that is meant to last for a long time (such as a business or school): a person who founds something, the founder of an empire."[39]

For years, driving around the rundown neighborhoods in the city where I worked, I wondered about the Crips. They were different than the rest of the gangs in our city. Now, many years later, after hearing the account of how the Crips actually formed, how they came to be called the Crips, I am amazed at how simple it all started. Who could have known what the outcome of this first meeting between two friends would be. The boys were classmates at 79th Street Elementary School, (See Pic 2-4) then junior high school, and later at Fremont High School. Just two inner-city kids that at first glance to anyone watching were really unremarkable. They would have looked like any two kids in any neighborhood in Los Angeles. Nothing special. But they were special, different somehow. Something about their two personalities was very different than the rest of the kids in Los Angeles. The way they clicked and talked to each other, the way their mutual experiences complemented each other and helped them to understand one another; Raymond Washington and Craig Craddock saw the world we all live in differently. Sitting on the front porch of Raymond's house, lifting weights in the garage, talking in the front room, boxing in the backyard, they formed the ideas, the culture, the dress code, the unique structure that would become the Crips. The talks began late in the fall of 1969; the gang would be formed and the two friends would set out on a mission to make a name for themselves, and their newly formed gang on the brutal streets of Los Angeles. The culture they formed would resonate throughout the inner city. It would eventually escape the confines of the inner city though, spreading across the country, and then across the world. Make no mistake about it, they formed a subculture that continues to grow today.

While we talked, Derard Barton told me, "I remember sitting there listening to Raymond and Craig talking. Raymond was going to form a gang. He had made his mind up, but he was searching for a name. He wanted something that was different, and they threw many names back and forth, listening to the different names as they spoke them out loud to each other. Raymond threw out the name 'Wildcats' and they mulled it over for a few minutes and then dismissed it. It had to be a name that would strike fear into the hearts of their enemies. When they really got the gang rolling and started to establish themselves in the street they wanted the entire city to know their name and fear it." So the two fifteen-year-old kids thought it over long and hard.

Derard said that, "Raymond was always sneaking in and borrowing our older brother Reggie's clothes. (See Pic 4-4) They were close in age and similar in size. So he would borrow Reggie's clothes when he was not around and wear them. While the two boys struggled with what name they should give their fledgling gang, Raymond looked down at the shoes he had borrowed from Reggie. There, written on the side of the Converse Chuck Taylor All Star shoe, was Reggie's nickname from the marching band he played in—'Crip.'"

According to Derard, "Raymond had an epiphany. His eyes opened wide, and he quietly said, 'Crip, we will name the gang the Crips.'" Repeating the name back and forth to each other, it grew on them. They sat down and formed the structure of the Crips. There would be many levels of Crips: Baby Crips, Crips, and Criplettes for the females who joined. I laughed at this initially, but I found many references to the Criplettes. They are mentioned in Greg Davis' book as he talks about a girl who headed up the Criplettes, Jackie, and her friend, Pam, and that they fought like the men with their rivals, the Bloods.

I asked Raymond's friend and neighbor, Raphael Pattaway, if he had any idea where the name of the Crips had originated. He confirmed, "Everyone that was there at the time the Crips started knew that the name came from his brother. Everyone that was in it from the start knew it." When I asked him if he knew which brother the name came from I did find it interesting that Raphael was not positive which brother.

When I asked John McDaniels if he knew the origin of the name, and if he knew what the reason behind the color choice was, he had his own version of events. He recalled two stories he had heard that accounted for the Crips having their name. The first story was the Avenues battle with Craig Munson, and the idea that Raymond had named the gang the Baby Avenues, which morphed into Baby Cribs and then—in McDaniels own words—"Raymond was uneducated, poorly spoken, and could not pronounce Cribs very well so it became Crips."

The second story McDaniels recalled was that one day while Raymond, Craig, and a few of their friends were hanging around at the back of Fremont High School, a woman walked by pushing a baby stroller. They watched her for a moment or two and then Raymond blurted out, "Let's call ourselves the Cribs." McDaniels was positive that one of these stories was the true origin for the name. While I appreciated McDaniels' trust and cooperation, these accounts made no sense. They do, however, add to the myth that surrounds the formation of the Crips and show that even the most senior members of the gang had no real understanding behind the choosing of the name. Thinking about this on a critical level, I wondered if Raymond had spread the false stories himself to protect his brother, Reggie, after the Crips grew and Reggie's life might have been in danger if the truth had ever been discovered. Raymond Washington was a master at creating and maintaining a mystical and mythical culture around himself and the Crips, and this account proved that to me even further.

Raymond and Craig established a dress code very early on that has morphed over the years. Initially the Crips were expected to dress and act in a very defined way. Some of it was adopted from the time Raymond spent in the Avenues, some of it was his and Craig Craddock's own ideas. Starting from the top and working down, Crips were expected to wear an Ace Deuce derby, and they would put matchsticks in the ribbon at the base of the hat. Later, they wore apple hats and golf hats.

Pants had to be khaki Levi's, tan or gray in color, with the suspenders hanging down, not blue jeans as is mentioned in Robert Stack's documentary *Lords of the Mafia: Raymond Lee Washington* (2004). If you wore a button-up shirt it had to be buttoned to the top. If you wore a T-shirt it had to be what is now colloquially known as a wife beater, or muscle T-shirt. Shoes worn were Crocus X, Romeos, or Biscuits made by Stacy Adams. The color of the leather shoes was tan as well. Crips wore an earring in the left ear, and would fly a blue flag (rag) in their left rear pocket. They would keep a pair of leather gloves in their front left pocket that they would take out and put on immediately before a fight. Everything was on the left side. Originally they walked with a cane and wore black leather jackets. Crips also had a distinct dancing style that became known as a Crip walk. It was originally much different than it is today and involved more "poppin' and lockin'," and some breakdance moves. Today it's a very distinct dance step unique to Crips such as the example of Snoop Dogg in the video for the song "Drop It Like It's Hot."[40] Ice Cube also did the "C walk," or "Crip walk."[41]

I asked Derard if he knew why Raymond chose the color blue for the gang's colors. He said, "At the time, Raymond wanted the gang to be different from every other gang. The Black Panthers had referred to each other as 'blood' as a sign of unity among black people. Raymond wanted to be different so he came up with the term 'Cuz.' Crips would refer to each other as Cuz, not blood. And since blood was identified with the color red, Raymond chose the color blue, simple as that. He wanted the Crips to stand out and be different from every other gang in the neighborhoods of South Central."

There are some stories on the web that there was a corner liquor store where everyone went to hang out, and that they sold two colors of the popular rags. One was blue and the other red. So when the time to choose a color came, Raymond had two choices. I cannot find any real proof of this story, however it is mentioned in the documentary by Robert Stack, *Lords of the Mafia: Raymond Lee Washington.*

Tony Craddock had his own comments on the color of the gang, and the origin of the term "Cuz." He said, "I don't know about where the name of the Crips originated from, but I do know this: there was a guy named Buck on the West side that was from Louisiana. He would always refer to people when he did not know their names as Cuz. Ya know, like cousin. He would say, 'Hey, Cuz, what's up, Cuz' and before you know it the Crips had adopted the term into their gang. Buck was a West side Crip and was nothing but a country brother who used the term over and over and it stuck with the Crips. As far as the color, it did not come into play until later on. When the gang started out there was Crips wearing red, and no one thought twice about it. The color was just not that big of a deal in the beginning."

John McDaniels had yet another version of how the color blue was chosen. I asked him directly if he knew, and he replied, "Hell ya I know, they came from our class color at Fremont High. Every class chose a different color as their own for graduation and that was the color we chose, powder blue. That was set back in 1969." Again, this only shows that there are many stories and myths surrounding the Crips and Raymond Washington. Each of the senior surviving members felt that they alone knew the truth. Somehow, Raymond was able to convince each of them that they alone held the secrets to the Crips. He made them all feel special. He was obviously very skilled at understanding what was required to win their unquestioning loyalty.

James Ward brought up another point concerning the confusion about the Crips versus Cribs, and where the name originated. Ward said, "I grew up next door to Raymond, and I knew that the name came from his big brother, Reggie. That was known earlier on. But we used to laugh at people who would write on the walls and spray paint names and stuff because they could not spell. There was a lot of people in L.A. from the South and they were poorly educated. So when they heard us mention the Crips, they thought we were saying Cribs, and they would write Cribs on the walls, but it was never ever the Cribs. Whoever tells you that really has no idea what they are talking about. It started as Crips and stayed that way, under one umbrella until the set tripping started. That was when it all went bad. People started claiming Hoover Crips, or 4trey Crips or Inglewood Crips, Compton Crips then it got ugly and Crips started going to war against Crips, killing each other." Reality was that the Crips had grown exponentially, and it would be nearly impossible to prevent fighting among such a large and diverse group. The Crips were growing daily and adding members that had no idea of the origin, the ideology and, more than likely, did not care.

Once the Crips were founded and the ideology was set, Raymond Washington and Craig Craddock started to recruit members. Their philosophy was simple yet effective. They would approach the leader of the gang they wanted to roll into the Crips, and ask him to join them. If he refused to join, they fought and took over the gang by force. If the gang members refused to join after the battle between Raymond Washington and their leader, they became enemies, and the Crips started to put in work against their set. The message was simple: join us, or fight for your lives. Not everyone joined, and the bloody battles for the streets of Los Angeles began in earnest.

Every one of the Crips I interviewed felt like they had special insight into Raymond's early life, or a story about Raymond Washington that no one had ever heard. Some really did have valuable insight that made me stop and take notice. Others knew a minor detail of an event that was special to them, but for the most part did not add much to flesh out the whole picture of who Raymond was as a person and how he thought.

In an article written in December of 2005 in the *LA Weekly*, Derard Barton is quoted as saying, "Raymond had a simple and very effective tactic of expanding the Crips. He would go to the leader of another gang and fight him. He went straight to their main man. Once he put the guy on his back, everyone else would join up and follow him." Los Angeles Police Detective Caffey agreed, saying, "He [Raymond] went to other neighborhoods and said, 'Either join me or become my enemy.'"[3]

Another story that Derard told me gave some insight into the defiant and indomitable spirit of Raymond Washington. Derard remembered one trip his mother made to visit Raymond in juvenile lockup. He said, "My mother went to visit Raymond in lockup, and she brought her boyfriend, Mr. Glaze, with her and they sat and talked with Raymond for a while." His mother recalled that as she left, Raymond made the remark that he would "see her at home." She thought nothing of it, but probably should have known that Raymond had some kind of plan in mind. She left the facility and drove home. As soon as she left, Raymond set his plan into motion. He escaped the correctional facility for juveniles and looked for an immediate and quick method to get out of the area. He later said that he saw a "white dude" on a motorcycle and took it from him, throwing him off the bike while he climbed on. Raymond had already started toward home while his mother had barely left the parking lot. Derard said that he was at home when Raymond came walking in the door. Surprised, he said, "Mom was supposed to be visiting you!" Raymond said that she had. Then his mother walked in and asked what he was doing there, and how he'd gotten home. According to Derard, Raymond replied, "I told you I would see you at home." (See Pic 3-1)

The first meeting of the original members of the Crips took place on the football field of Fremont High School at 7676 South San Pedro Street in Los Angeles. As the gang grew, the bleachers on the football field would fill-up with members. Members from all of the sets on the East side would show up and discuss their strategy and goals for the next week. Who to put in work on next, who to rob, where to steal and store weapons and ammunition. "Green lights," or "assassination orders," were put out on enemies who were deemed a threat, or who had disrespected the gang. The table-top tactical exercises of Raymond Washington's childhood were bearing real and tangible fruit as he expanded the criminal enterprise that the Crips would become. Later as the gang grew, meetings would be held in other places that were large enough to include the growing membership. This included parks and high school football fields.

There is a famous murder that occurred in Hollywood in 1972. It is known as the first documented homicide by the Crips. Robert Brooks Ballou was allegedly beaten and killed for his leather jacket after attending a concert by the group War. Ballou was seventeen-years-old. Four men were convicted for his murder at that time. They were listed as James "Cuz" Cunningham, Ricardo "Bub" Sims, Big Bob the Hawk, and Judson Bacot.

There is some controversy as to whether the media got the story right or not. In an interview conducted by Alex Alonso, founder of *streetgangs.com*, you can watch the claims made by Big Bob and Judson Bacot after their release from prison for the Ballou murder.[42] Their account is much different than the official one, and most likely false. They claim to have been setup, and that the court ignored the facts of the case. In my experience, judges don't ignore facts that come into their courtroom. Period. If the facts never make it into the courtroom, that is another issue. In this case they did.

There have been many Crip gang members that have made the claim that they were founders, or founding members. None were present at this first Crips meeting of the two founders of the Crips.

The *Learners Dictionary* defines a founding member as, "an original member of a group."[43] In this context, claims made by several famous and/or infamous Crip gang members would be accurate. They were original members, they joined the Crips early on, and bought into the culture and code of conduct that Raymond Washington and Craig Craddock were instrumental in "founding." Stanley Williams, Greg Davis, John McDaniels, Marcus Jones, Michael Concepcion, and Jimel Barnes were all original members. None, however, were founders. According to Alex Alonso, "All this talk of Stanley 'Tookie' Williams being the co-founder of the Crips is a lot of embellishment because there is no doubt Raymond Washington founded the Crips." Even Wes McBride, president of the California Gang Investigators Association is quoted as saying, "It's just wrong to say Tookie was the founder of the Crips."[3]

Raymond was also recognized as the sole founder by *PBS.org* in the documentary *Crips and Bloods: Made in America*.[44]

Additionally, in John Irwin's book, *Lifers: Seeking Redemption in Prison*, John interviewed a member of the Crips that had grown up on the East side of South Central Los Angeles. The man used the pseudonym "Jerry" during the interview. He mentioned that it was common knowledge that Raymond Washington was the founder of the Crips. (2010, pp. 21-22)

The documentary, *Crips and Bloods: Made in America*, narrated by Forest Whitaker, also acknowledged that, "In the late 1960s on the black-top playgrounds of Fremont High School emerged this new order, led by South L.A. teenager Raymond Washington, generally credited as the Crips founding member."

Donald Bakeer wrote a book based on the real life events in South Central. The book is listed as historical fiction, but specifically mentions on the cover that he tried to, "Capture the spirit of the OGs, and specifically the spirit of the founder of the Crips, Raymond Washington." (1999)

Clearly some of the mainstream media missed this small detail in the winter of 2005 as Williams' execution was approaching, and later in the publishing of *Blue Rage, Black Redemption* (2007) by Stanley "Tookie" Williams. But why let the truth get in the way of a good story? As I mentioned earlier, in the interview by Alex Alonso, two members of the West side Crips talk about the murder of Robert Ballou. They make several claims about the incident that have been debated in the mainstream media. What I thought was interesting, however, was the fact that they made the claim that there was no single leader of the Crips. They say that the Crips were just a bunch of gangs that were loosely affiliated and that no one person was in charge. They go on to say that when there was a Crips meeting "you had better send someone to represent" your set. There were Crips meetings that alternated from the East side to West side of South Central Los Angeles. The original dividing line was Main Street, but has now switched to the 110 Harbor Freeway.

My cop listening skills kicked in when I heard this. Interviewing and interrogation is as much about listening to what is not being said as it is to listening to what is. Those being interviewed claimed that there were weekly and sometimes bi-weekly meetings of the East and West side Crips. That implies organization and a communications network within all of the sets. If there were no leaders, as these two older Crips members claimed, who called the meetings, and why was it so important to represent your set at the meetings if no one was in charge?

Clearly someone was in charge. Someone that they feared, and respected. Someone whose reputation on the streets was so fearsome it would make known murderers, thugs, and criminals stand up and take notice. They knew they had better be there at the meetings or they would answer to whoever the leader was. It is highly doubtful in my mind that they feared a ghost or a figment of someone's imagination. They feared Raymond Washington and the power he held within the Crips.

CHAPTER FIVE

POWER OF MYTH AND THE CRIPS

There are two questions that social scientists, psychologists, sociologists, people in law enforcement, and government leaders at the local state and federal levels all ask when it comes to the growing problem of gangs worldwide. Why do people join a gang, and what can we do to stop it?

One of the common misconceptions about why people join gangs is the idea that they are just looking for family, and a place to feel loved and belong. This explanation never rang true for me. Gang life is anything but a loving and nurturing environment. So the question remains, why do they join?

I have studied gangs for nearly twenty years off and on as a cop, and as a gang detective. I attended the California Gang Conferences, and the Office of Juvenile Justice seminars in Dallas, Texas, looking for a plausible answer to this question. I have read every book I can find, written by authors on all sides of the problem. I could never find an answer that satisfied me as to why gangs, specifically gangs like the Crips and Sur 13, continue to grow and flourish. Legislators have added more laws to the books, gang injunctions have been passed prohibiting gang members from assembling in groups larger than three people. Youth programs have been funded, sports programs, educational programs, parenting programs. Yet nothing seems to slow the growth of gangs in our culture. What were they all missing?

Thinking that these alleged experts have a handle on what being in a gang means to the gang members would be a huge mistake. They most definitely don't understand anything about it. I have attended seminars where a psychologist and academic in good standing with the Office of Juvenile Justice made the argument that gang members were just average people who had been robbed of their childhood. Her theory—which was widely accepted and praised at the time—was that if gang members could be allowed to "re-experience" childhood by playing on swings and monkey bars, playing kickball and kick-the-can, even crawling around on the floor like babies (no shit, she actually said this), they would be able to form healthier coping mechanisms, and no longer need their gang membership.

I sat in the back of the session, speechless, listening to these educated idiots praise each other for their intuition and insight into the real issues that caused gang members to join the gang. I thought to myself, *No fucking wonder nothing gets done about gangs. If these idiots are the leaders in their field, we are all screwed.* To be honest, this sounded more like some weird sexual fantasy the "expert" in question had dreamt up than any real problem-solving therapy. I got up and left that seminar, listening to the filled auditorium explode with enthusiastic clapping and shouts of praise for the amazing insight the audience had just been given.

I would love to see what Raymond Washington would have thought about this concept. I can imagine him looking at me, eyes wide, and eyebrows raised, speechless as we shared the unspoken thought, *Are these idiot motherfuckers for real?* Yes they are, very real. It's no wonder that gang members worldwide see them as marks, ripe for robbing of their belongings, victims to be taken advantage of. They don't live in the real world of the streets, they are set apart and much too different to understand what the gang is to the gang member.

Law enforcement has a more visceral and thug-like approach, which, I discovered after being assigned to the Gang Unit of the department I worked for, is equally as unrealistic as the view adopted by those in academia. We were taught early on the only way to successfully deal with gangs was to be as aggressive as was possible, and still be able to legally get away with it. We were taught to use intimidation, to harass them, and make their lives hell. It would never work. Gang members do not have to play by the rules of our country's constitution, and they have not sworn an oath to protect the laws and ideas our country is founded on. They are outside of that idea. They have no rules except their own code of conduct, made up as they go along.

Our job was to make it as uncomfortable for them to be in the city as was legally possible. This philosophy is used by police departments all over, and is still very much in place today. It never worked for me, although I will admit there were some gangs that we took apart piece by piece. We basically dismantled them, removing the leaders and the shot callers through informants, and using the correctional system to get them off the street temporarily. It did work from our point of view, much like a Band-Aid works when you need a tourniquet. It was a temporary fix to a long-term problem. Gang members were locked up, and when they returned, they had been "trained up" in the jails and prison system. They came out fitter, smarter, and hell bent on making a mark in the streets. We just fueled the fire that made them want to be in their particular gangs.

On a rare occasion, some gang members came back to the world changed and wanted to go straight, or "retire" from the set. Notice I said, "retire." Every single gang member I have ever spoken with has told me unequivocally that they regret the people they harmed, and the evil deeds and/or bad things they may have done, but they did not for one minute regret their time spent in the gang. Think about that for a minute. What are we missing here as outside observers?

I finally had my epiphany reading *The Power of Myth* (2011), by Joseph Campbell. The concept was so incredibly simple, and yet had been missed the world over by every academic leader, every law enforcement official, and every civic leader who had ever wondered what do we do about the gang problem. Campbell spoke with journalist Bill Moyers about the need for societies to have cultural myths, traditions, and rituals that applied to the times. In a very brief synopsis of the conversation that Moyers and Campbell had, Campbell outlines the reason for the majority of the violence, and the reason for joining gangs: our society has no traditions or rituals by which children can become members of our adult society. He claimed that there is no transition from girl to woman, boy to man. He said that when kids have no traditions, they make them up on their own, outside of society.

Here is the excerpt that I believe addressed the issue with such incredible clarity:

Moyers: Where do kids growing up in the city, on 125 and Broadway, (Or South Central Los Angeles in Raymond Washington's case) where do they get their myth today?

Campbell: They make them up themselves. This is why we have graffiti all over the city. These kids have their own gangs and their own initiations and their own morality and they are doing the best they can. But they're dangerous because their own laws are not those of the city. They have not been initiated into our society.

Moyers: Rollo May says there is so much violence in American society today because there are no great myths to help young men and women relate to the world or to understand that world beyond what is seen.

Campbell: Yes, but another reason for the high level of violence here is that America has no ethos.

Moyers: Explain.

Campbell: In American football for example the rules are very strict and complex. If you were to go to England, however, you would find that the rugby rules are not that strict. When I was a student in my twenties, there were a couple of men who constituted a marvelous forward passing pair. They went to Oxford on scholarship and joined the rugby team and one day introduced the forward pass. And the English players said well we have no rules for this so please don't. We don't play that way."

Moyers: A mythology.

Campbell: An unstated mythology, you might say. This is the way we use a fork and knife, this is the way we deal with people and so forth. It is not all written down in books. But in America we have people from all kinds of backgrounds all in a cluster, together, and consequently law has become very important to us. Lawyers and the law are what hold us together. There is no ethos. What we have today is a demythologized world.

This conversation rang true to me in a way I have never been able to quite explain until I started doing the research for this book.

So what exactly did Raymond do when he formed the Crips that so resonated with people? It crossed economic and cultural boundaries. Rich and poor, educated and uneducated alike, identify with their time spent as Crips. Why is that? What is it that a poor, inner-city kid shares with a wealthy, protected, and pampered kid from the suburbs? What is it that makes them want to join this gang or identify with its members? The need is so strong that they would rather join and put their lives and families' lives at risk, rather than sit on the sidelines. What do they see in being a member that the academics and law enforcement don't understand?

The Crips spread across Los Angeles, and then broke out of the confines of South Central and spread across the entire North American continent. Some forty-five years later, they continue to thrive. I believe the reason behind this is simple. Raymond Washington and Craig Craddock provided a mechanism for gang members to be initiated into a subculture. That subculture had a set of rules and initiations, a style of dress, a way to walk, talk, and dance and be identified as a group. There is an unspoken ethos here that is lacking in traditional, accepted cultures across the planet. Kids that are outside the societal norms look for a place to fit in, a way to be indoctrinated and accepted. Not because they have bad parents, or dysfunctional families, but because humans on a gut level need the traditions, rituals, and myths that used to be a part of primitive culture. We have replaced them with laws, lawyers, and court systems. The modern day thought is that right and wrong are black and white, written in a court document or a book of codes of law set down by the legislature. It is not passed on by accepted norms and ethos.

The evidence for this is in the way that Raymond Washington established the Crips.

- There was an established dress code in the gang. An established manner of speaking to and identifying each other. The use of the blue rags, hand signs, and terminology like "Cuz"' instead of "Blood" as had been used by the Black Panthers.

- Gang members had to go through an initiation process, either a fight or a beat down, or committing some sort of crime.
- There were well-documented meetings held regularly to reinforce the ethos of the gang, and give clear direction to the gang's members. Membership was required to attend these meetings.
- There was an expected loyalty and toughness that had to be proven repeatedly in the street and in the gang warfare. These types of life and death battles test the character and mettle of the individual—much like the battles in World War I and II, Vietnam, and more recently, Afghanistan and Iraq. Gang members exhibit the same type of regret for the human cost that war exacts, but they also define those moments as being the times they felt closest to their comrades in arms, or "homies" as the gang members refer to each other.

This membership has nothing to do with dysfunction. It has everything to do with being a human. I have a friend who strongly identifies with her alma mater, The University of Washington. She is a die-hard Husky fan, and recently the Huskies' long-term football coach left the team for another position. She had worshiped the coach, and what he had done for the team during his tenure. She was so disappointed in the coach when he took a better job she posted on the web, "Coach Sarkisian is dead to me from now on."

She very much identified with the myth, tradition, and ethos that came with her time spent at Washington State University, in spite of graduating from the college fifteen years ago. Consider this: where do the "outliers" in society go to get that sense of belonging all humans need?

An "outlier" is defined as: "a person or thing situated away or detached from the main body or system."

Isn't that description exactly what Joseph Campbell is talking about when he mentions young adults who have no rituals, myth, or tradition to help them find their way and role in mainstream society? That is exactly what Raymond Washington's culture of the Crips provided, and, just as Campbell predicted, "they form gangs and are dangerous."

Here it is again:

> *Moyers: Where do kids growing up in the city, on 125 and Broad-*
> *way, (Or South Central Los Angeles in Raymond Washington's case)*
> *where do they get their myth today?*
> *Campbell: They make them up themselves. This is why we have*
> *graffiti all over the city. These kids have their own gangs and their*
> *own initiations and their own morality and they are doing the best*
> *they can. But they're dangerous because their own laws are not those*
> *of the city. They have not been initiated into our society.*

A former Slauson Street gang member, Kumasi Washington, explained how he saw the kids that became Crips gang members in Raymond Washington's era, and I believe it supports what Joseph Campbell has described. Here is the quote from that video: "They were born in a state of suspended animation. They were totally disconnected and disenfranchised, they were like a planet out of orbit." [33]

John Amos and Mike "Shaft" Concepcion thought that they could replace this culture with a three-day boating trip, and at the end of the three days, Crips and Bloods would be singing campfire songs and making s'mores.[34] That's never going to happen. Not in the real world. You cannot replace an entire subculture with a brief trip to *Fantasy Island* while you eat some fucking s'mores, and sing campfire songs. Who in their right mind would believe this?

Raymond Washington lived what Joseph Campbell had so clearly understood at an intellectual level. He had watched the Black Panther Party leaders in his neighborhood murdered by fellow black activists in the US organization. He had also watched the Watts riots from a front row seat and ventured out into the night to obtain sporting goods equipment from a nearby store. He knew what it meant to need to belong to something and yet have nothing that fit his needs. A warrior mentality burned into his soul; he could not pretend to be a sheep and follow the rules of society. He made his own rules, his own myth, and his own ethos. For better or worse, he formed the Crips and set fire to the imaginations of kids all across the country and eventually the world.

James Ward did an outstanding job of describing this mentality to me as we talked. He said, "I had to move from Los Angeles after a while because you know I had been doing my thing and people were looking for me hard. My mom moved me with my dad to keep me alive, so I went to stay with my dad in Kansas City. You know you can take a person out of the hood, I mean you can remove them from the environment, but you can't take the hood out of the person. All my mother did was to transport the things I was doing in Los Angeles and move them to Kansas City. It did not slow me down one bit. I got to Kansas City and ran into a homeboy from the West side of Los Angeles, and we started Crippin there. I was always trying to keep up that militant mentality from the Panthers and try to make sure that I looked out for my boys and my younger family members. That loyalty would get me into a lot of trouble."

He continued, "You know, for example, in one school there might be four or five different gangs, and so you were always trying to keep your gang on top. You had to be always making sure that anyone who challenged you or your homies got a response. If you failed to represent your gang properly and let their rep slide, that was when the real problems started. You could never show any sign of weakness, ever! So you had to make sure that your hood was always staying on top. The girls were putting in work as well. They did as much for the reputation of the set as we did. At first they were less lethal than the men and they had the name in the set as Criplettes. Later on, though, they were just Crips, they would get down with the guys, fight, carry guns, doing it all. I am telling you, you had to be watching your ass with the women because they would set your ass up and get you killed!"

I was surprised to find many examples of the warrior mentality exhibited by Raymond Washington and Craig Craddock in many kids their age and younger. Here are a few of the examples I found in more traditional and less criminal paths:

- James R. Clark enlisted in the army at thirteen years of age to fight in WWII.[45]
- Calvin Graham enlisted in the navy at twelve years of age during WWII.[46]
- Jack Lucas enlisted at age fourteen into WWII and became the youngest marine to receive the Medal of Honor.[47]

- Audie Murphy enlisted at age eighteen, and became the most decorated American veteran ever.[48]

Looking at these examples, you can see that at a very young age they all felt the need to be tested in combat, and to belong to a specific culture (military and/or gangs). They had a sense of ethos and wanted to do what they could for their country (or neighborhood). Each was profoundly affected by the experience of battle. There are many interesting parallels between the accounts of these war heroes and the actions of Raymond Washington. One glaring problem with these mainstream stories is that they did not commit crimes. They lived within the norms of society, bought into the societal norms, and became acclimated into the society. Raymond Washington did not, but still he felt the need to do battle with an enemy, belong to a group, protect his neighborhood, and make a name for himself. Even more than that, he needed to lead. Leadership was a large part of who he was. He refused to follow anyone blindly.

I contacted three friends who at one time were adversaries of mine. Each are Crips gang members from the city I worked in. One had roots in the Crips at an early age and later joined a local gang that was headed up by a formidable leader, who was very much like Raymond Washington. The other joined the set that was in his neighborhood, a first generation Crip. I asked each for his take on what it meant to him to belong to the Crips, what it was about "Crippin" that appealed to him. They each thought about it for several days, and then responded with the following:

Travis "Sandman" Elliot had this to say: "You asked me what it meant to me, Crippin. It took me a minute but we could have been Blood, Sur 13s, Moon Dawgs...shit even GDs (Gangster Disciples)... Honestly it was our love and loyalty, our friendship bonds that have lasted twenty-plus years. Our hood was never bigger than us if you know what I'm trying to say." He continued, "Crippin ain't easy but damn sho fun. That's what we always say, that and, now I lay me down too sleep, I tie blue rags around my feet, if I should die C-for I wake I'm a smoke me a slob (Blood) wit a .38...terrible but powerful words."[36]

Mike S. aka "Snoop" had this to say (unedited): "I don't have a long sob story of having a hard life that pushed me to the gang life. Actually, my parents were great and they raised me well. The fact is, I was just always drawn towards the gang lifestyle. I can't explain it. The camaraderie, the violence, and the power was magnetic. I didn't start gang banging because I wanted to be a Crip. I did it because I wanted to bang with the big boys and the neighborhood I got put on just happened to be a Crip set. My mentality changed immediately after I got jumped in. I became a different person. I flew my colors daily and if someone asked me where I was from I told them. Fucc slobs was the motto. Fucc 'em all. That's what I signed up for and there ain't no turning back. Throughout the years it wasn't just the Piru's though, it was anyone and everyone that had a problem with me or my neighborhood. Didn't matter if it was Crip, Blood, 13s, 14s, 18s, if you weren't from our side or you were disrespecting the team you were the enemy. My neighborhood wasn't the biggest and none of us cared. We were all tight and had each other's back, that's all that mattered.

"I felt invincible at times, but throughout the years you always seem to get a good reality checc every now and then to keep you in line which typically came by way of a good ass whoopin' or bullet wound. Somehow I managed to stay alive...

"20 years later I'm still the same guy I've always been, just smarter. I know a lot of dudes that are Crips and Bloods and I got respect for all of them. I don't get caught up in colors (blue and red) no more. Colors don't define who you are. I'll always stayed true to my roots and I'm proud of where I'm from. Bottom line is, all the violence I've been through has made me a stronger person and I wouldn't be who I am without it."[49]

Finally, Jason Tafoya, the single most formidable gang leader I personally ever faced as a cop said this some fifteen years after he too decided the life of a gang leader had taken enough of a toll on his own life: "It has been fifteen years since the decision was made. You see, Zach, the only way I ever understood anything was with action. I was never raised in a gang. I took the life of gang life seriously. Every little thing I do is intense and serious. Only reason for OVG or any other reason of foolishness was because other gangs was bullies, so we had to protect ourselves. Always wanted the dream. Never expected the results I faced and still face today. It is a shame to know how much of wasted lives and life has been sacrificed for unknown and lost reasons.

"You see, the mind is a washy form to trust. Emotions keep the wondering controllable. I never meant to take from anyone or harm anyone whom didn't deserve it. I remember all the whys. Why I lived and loved the lifestyle, character, power, can't deny even the strength, behind bars of a confined mind. Never expected to be around and free at this age. Yet alone having technology as a way to socialize. Have to admit, it feels good to be here."

I think these conversations speak volumes to the validity of the claim by Joseph Campbell in *The Power of Myth* about the lack of belonging to traditional society and the consequences. There is much about gang membership that has not been understood by academics and law enforcement. Where else besides combat can you forge relationships like these that stand the test of time?

Twice I would visit Los Angeles to meet with Derard Barton and his mother while doing research for this book. Both trips were interesting and eye opening. During one trip, I pulled up to a stoplight on Slauson Avenue. I was playing my favorite CD by Rage Against the Machine, Zach De La Rocha was belting out a hate-filled rant about oppressed people called "Wake Up" while I played my mock drums on my steering wheel. Then my whole car started to vibrate from the unmistakable bass of a killer stereo.

A low rider pulled up next to me with a huge man at the wheel. He was wearing a blue rag on his head, and had muscular arms the size of my legs hanging out the window as he surveyed the area. I saw that an elderly man, maybe eighty-five years old, was crossing the street. Due to his age and frail condition, I doubted that he would cross in the time allotted by the traffic light that governed the intersection. He did not make it and the monster in the car next to me yelled out in a deep menacing voice, "old man, get over here." The old man flinched, and a fearful look came over his face as he walked toward the now silent and glaring monster in the car next to me. I thought as I watched, *This is gonna suck, I don't want to get out here and deal with this poor ole man and this huge Dew Rag wearing apparently angry "OG."* I turned down my music, and pulled up the emergency brake as the angry guy sitting in his car next to me turned down his music as well. As the old man approached, the man in the car reached across the front seat to pick something up. I had no idea what to expect, thinking, *This is going to shit in a hurry.* He turned toward the elderly man, smiled, and gave him a meal in a take-out container, complete with napkin, and plastic spoon and fork. I was stunned. I watched as he wished the old man well and sent him on his way, tottering feebly across the remainder of the intersection. The formerly angry man looked directly at me, his eyes and facial features were now softer as we made eye contact. He nodded at me, smiling, and I returned the nod in appreciation for what I had just witnessed. This was not what I expected to see in South Central Los Angeles, on Slauson Avenue, no less. But I had witnessed it, and I made a point of noting where I was so that I could add this to the book. I continued on to Derard Barton's home, and we spoke about Raymond.

Another day I was headed to Lincoln Cemetery in Compton. I could see ahead of me a police helicopter circling a block. I knew I would have to drive through that area. I saw police squad cars parked on the side of the road at angles I recognized as ways to tactically approach a dangerous scene. The local police were out on foot, guns drawn and edgy as they waited, maintaining a tight perimeter around the scene. I watched as a woman walked past one cop who was directly in front of me with a small child in tow. The cop waved his gun in her direction and screamed at her to get back. Holding the gun like it was some kind of talisman, stuffed with the magic that would protect him while he was out of the patrol car. It was an odd contradiction, these two incidents, and I was to be reminded of them over and over again while I researched Raymond Washington. There was a weird duality to both the area in which he lived and the man. Nothing about the area he had lived in was what I expected; likewise, nothing about his character and personality were what I expected either.

CHAPTER SIX

THE CRIPS RISING

"The successful warrior is the average man, with laser-like focus."
~ Bruce Lee ~

"Every normal man must be tempted, at times, to spit on his hands, hoist the black flag, and begin slitting throats."
~ H.L. Mencken ~

Several accounts here describe various aspects of Raymond Washington's personality. Some provide insight into the side of his personality that was a mentor and fostered a religious-like loyalty among the Crips that still exists today. Others describe a tactician and warrior whose brutality and ruthlessness were, and still are, whispered about in the streets of Los Angeles. Surprisingly, still others detail acts of kindness to rivals that are almost impossible to believe, and yet I heard them over and over from independent sources. Raymond was seen as a protector by many in the neighborhood he lived in, but in the same breath those people would say he could also be a bully. I found accounts of LAPD officers who remembered Raymond as polite and friendly when they spoke to him. They did not have the same fondness for Stanley Williams; they described him as always being an "ignorant ass." They claimed that you could never talk to him.

It should be remembered that Raymond had learned early on to compartmentalize his life and behaviors. No one person knew everything there was to know about Raymond, except perhaps Craig Craddock, and even then I am not sure. Raymond was a very dynamic and charismatic leader who only showed the bare minimum of himself to enlist you into following his lead. That could be amazing courage, or incredible violence. If I were asked which of the following accounts were true, I would say all of them. At one time or another all were true.

"All warfare is based on deception."
~ Sun Tzu, *The Art of War* ~

One other fact that you should consider when you try to see why Raymond was so successful at gang leadership is that he did it for a very long time. He led the Crips fairly consistently for ten years. That is a magical number according to psychologist K. Anders Ericsson. Ericsson did a study that looked at what it took to achieve world-class expertise in any one area. In the study it was discovered that in almost every situation where someone had achieved a level of world-class excellence in a chosen field, it took approximately ten years of practice. This was known as the "ten thousand hour rule." (Gladwell, 2008) There are other factors that determine whether or not a person will succeed, such as talents, abilities, and hard work. I think that it is obvious from what I have discovered about Raymond Washington that he was immensely talented and driven, and he applied those gifts for the magical ten thousand hours needed. Raymond led the Crips of Los Angeles for exactly ten years (nearly to the exact day the Crips were founded).

Additionally, in the book *Leadership Secrets of Attila the Hun,* written by Wess Roberts, PhD, the traits of exceptional leaders are discussed in great length. One single passage stood out to me as it pertains to Raymond Washington and the obvious many extremes of his personality and leadership style: "you must recognize that your greatness will be made possible by the *extremes* of your personality—the very extremes that sometimes make for campfire satire and legendary stories." By the time Raymond Washington was through with his life, and leading the Crips, there would be many legendary stories.

RAYMOND AS A PROTECTOR

"Don't mistake my kindness for weakness. I am kind to everyone, but when someone is unkind to me, weak is not what you are going to remember about me."
~ Al Capone ~

Violet Samuel remembers her son fondly. She said that Raymond, "Spent a lot of time looking out for the neighborhood, and that he made sure we were safe. If Raymond found out anyone in the neighborhood had a problem he took care of it, no matter what it was." She explained that if someone was being harassed by drug addicts or thugs Raymond made it stop immediately.

This statement was supported by Derard. He said, "While Raymond was leading the Crips and in full power and control of the East side of Los Angeles, no one had their homes broken into for several blocks around our house...period! No one dared to enter the territory claimed by him, and if they did Raymond quickly took care of it. He kept us all safe." (See Pics 5-3, 5-4)

James Ward said, "People have painted Raymond Washington as a monster, but he wasn't. He was a cool cat, he was all about helping his friends, and he was really down to earth. If he saw that you would stand up for yourself to anyone, no matter who they were or how big, he would have love for you. But if you didn't, if you was a punk, Raymond had no time for you, and he would tell you straight up you are a punk get the hell out of my face. He was like that, very direct, and very down to earth."

Raphael Pattaway remembered Raymond in a similar manner. He said, "A lot of the old stories that people told about Raymond, they never told the good things, like he would come by and stop and talk to our mom and everyone else's mom. They would feed him, and they loved him! He would just stop and talk to them and make sure that they were doing okay. People tell stories that he was vicious and crazy like some madman maniac and started all this nonsense. He wasn't. He looked out for us. There were a lot of times he diffused some situations, like one time some guys came over to a friend's house and stole some hydraulic motors that you would use to put in low riders. My friend wasn't home and when he found out about it he went and got Raymond and told him what happened. Raymond got everyone together and we all went over there and got the stuff back, without a fight. Simple as that, because Raymond liked to solve things without a fight if he could. It was like this, if Raymond was there to talk you had better listen, because you did not want him there to fight. That could get real ugly, real fast."

Ray Rhone told me during our interview that, "The Crips were originally formed to protect the neighborhood." I asked him what they were protecting it from, and he said, "In the 1960s the cops would come into the neighborhoods and beat the hell out of people, and then there were white people that had gangs that would drive around and if they caught you they would do things to you. You couldn't call the cops because they wouldn't do anything, so after the Panthers collapsed, the Crips were formed to protect the neighborhood. At least that was how it started. I don't know how it got so out of hand. I moved away to the West side so I missed that part."

Hearing about this side of Raymond was difficult for me to accept. As a cop working in a city ravaged by gang violence it was hard to believe that the original founder and leader of the Crips actually "protected" his neighborhood. We felt like we protected the neighborhoods from the gangs and tried to make the residents feel safe. In actuality, we went to war with the Crips in our city, drawing a line in the proverbial sand. The idea of the founder of the Crips protecting his hood was very hard to accept. After the research and interviewing I did, I had to accept that this, too, was a part of Raymond Washington. If you were his friend and ally there was nothing he would not do for you. If you were an enemy, however, there was nothing he was not capable of doing to defeat you.

RAYMOND AS A WARRIOR/TACTICIAN

> *"Don't hit a man if you can possibly avoid it;*
> *but if you do hit him, put him to sleep."*
> ~ Theodore Roosevelt— New York City, 17 February, 1899 ~

The first myth I heard when I started researching Raymond was that he hated to use weapons and preferred to fight hand-to-hand. It's true that he did make a name initially for himself as an accomplished brawler in the streets. His street fighting prowess was legendary, and many of his friends and followers to this day maintain that he could have taken on anyone, literally anyone in the world, and won in a street fight. He was alleged to have a wickedly effective and brutal left hook, and as a left-handed fighter I am sure that he had an advantage against the predominately right-handed population.

Additionally, he worked out feverishly; power lifting in his own personal gym, which he maintained in the garage at his mother's house. Weight lifting, boxing, and training were a huge part of his life, and as his brother Derard told me, "Raymond would make me and my friends box in the backyard for hours. We would have to fight until we were exhausted and our arms ached. We would take a break for a few moments and then Raymond would tell us to get back in there. Raymond told me that he wanted me to be tough and to be able to take care of myself, but it wasn't just me that he looked after. It was all the neighborhood kids. If Raymond liked you, even if you were quite a bit younger, he would go to your house and ask your parents if you could come out and play football in the streets with us. He was always very respectful if he liked you. If he thought you were a punk or a bitch, you might want to move out of the neighborhood as quickly as possible."

Hearing that Raymond preferred to fight hand-to-hand was a direct contradiction to another couple of stories that Derard told me while we talked about Raymond in the early spring of 2014. Derard said that he remembered after his mother went to work, Craig Craddock would come over to the house and lay out two handguns on the table, and ask Raymond which gun he wanted to use for the day. This was immediately after the Crips had been formed and much more in-line with the reality of the streets of Los Angeles at the time.

James Ward also recalled, "Every morning Raymond and Craig Craddock, sometimes Tookie Williams would be there, but mostly it was Raymond and Craig. They would go to the garage behind the house and clean guns. They were always cleaning the guns to be ready to go!"

You did not show up to a gunfight with only your fists or a knife. Not if you wanted to survive longer than the time it took to pull the trigger. You had better bring your "A" game and be prepared to do battle on many different levels. I personally think this quote says it best:

"Don't get set into one form, adapt it and build your own, and let it grow, be like water."
~ Bruce Lee ~

This could not have been lost on Raymond Washington or Craig Craddock. They entered the streets after forming the Crips with a working knowledge of the rules of engagement that governed the gang warfare in Los Angeles. Be formless, and adapt to the moment, and you will survive. The strongest, smartest, and most lethal warriors lived to see the next day. The rest were just victims waiting to be put down, hoping to avoid the killers that patrolled the streets. I think this quote I found by another infamous gangster explains it best:

"You can get a lot farther with a kind word and a gun than a kind word alone."
~ Al Capone ~

Another story that Derard recalled vividly shows the incredible luck and stubbornness Raymond possessed. He refused to be dominated or defeated by anyone. Derard said, "I remember playing in the street out in front of the house one day with a friend, and Raymond came driving around the corner in a Chevy Monza. The tires were screeching as the car made the sharp corner, barely under control. The wheels looked funny, like they were bent in as Raymond pulled up to the house and jumped out of the car and ran inside. I ran up to the car and there were bullet holes all over it. I later found out that Raymond had been in a gunfight with the Figueroa boys." (A rival gang that would eventually be rolled into the Crips under Raymond's iron fist. They are named after the street they reside on—Figueroa Street.)

Raymond had escaped the attack somehow unharmed but determined that he would answer the attack and leave no doubt as to the outcome of challenging his position. Derard said, "Raymond came running out of the house a few moments later with a shotgun. He jumped back into the bullet-riddled car and sped off down the street to gather up more Crips, and then went back at the Figueroa boys. I had no idea what happened then, but it could not have been pretty."

These accounts directly contradict the accounts given by Greg Davis in his book. He recalls showing Raymond he had a shotgun as they were walking one day and that Raymond was upset with him for carrying the weapon and admonished him, saying, "No, we fight with our fists." Clearly guns were used in the Crips' battles for dominance of the streets of Los Angeles early on.

Alex Alonso agreed with Greg Davis in that weapons were not used early on in the gang's warfare. He states it was not until later, when cocaine entered the streets (the mid-'90s), and gangs began getting involved in the drug trade, that the real use of guns began.

Los Angeles County Sheriff gang unit personnel strongly disagree with both Greg Davis and Alex Alonso. They state that guns were widely in use early on in gang warfare. To me this makes sense when you listen to the eyewitness accounts of Derard Barton and also take into account the murders of Black Panther leaders Bunchy Carter and John Huggins. Guns were clearly in play early on. Additionally, take a close look at the left hand of Raymond Washington in Pic 5-3. He is holding a snub-nosed revolver. How averse could he really have been to using guns?

I asked Derard where Raymond kept the guns in the house, and if they were left out in the open in his room. He laughed, and said, "No, our mother would never have allowed him to have guns in the house, and he knew it. She would have raised all kinds of hell if she knew about any guns being in the house, so he had to hide them." He continued, "I looked in the house time and time again for the guns, and I could never find where he hid them. I looked in the attic, and under his bed, in his closet, everywhere I could think of, and I never found a single handgun or shotgun. When he needed them, he would tell me to go outside and then he would come out with a gun he had hidden somewhere. I don't know where he hid them, and I never found out. To this day that still remains a mystery."

There is a lot about Raymond that remains a mystery, and his myth continues to grow. Marcus Jones recalled a nearly fatal battle that he and Raymond were both involved in early on. He said that Raymond had led a small group of neighborhood kids into a rival neighborhood's turf. They were headed into a Florence 13 neighborhood. The Florence 13 is a Hispanic gang that still exists today and has a long, proud history of gang activity in Los Angeles.[50]

Raymond had targeted a rival's house deep inside the gang's territory and led a small group of approximately ten guys through the back alleys and hidden trails until they arrived at the rear of the home. They began throwing rocks and bottles at the home, breaking windows and taunting the occupants, daring them to come out and face them. Raymond had assumed that they had traveled unnoticed and had caught the neighborhood and occupants of the home unaware. This was not the case, and the Florence 13 set were about to respond to the incursion, but they would do it tactically.

While the group led by Raymond continued to pelt the home with rocks and bricks and bottles, Florence 13 were setting up a trap. They started by showing a large force of gang members at one end of the alleyway occupied by Raymond and his group. The Florence 13 members had bats, chains, and knives visible and at the ready as they closed on the smaller group. Raymond announced it was time to "get the fuck out of here," and the group took off running as fast as they could toward the opposite end of the alleyway.

It was a hot summer afternoon in South Central, the heavy foot traffic of the rapid exodus had stirred up a lot of dust and the now fearful and sweat-covered group were also covered in the dust of the alleyway. Just as it looked like they would make their escape and exit the Florence 13 territory unharmed, another large group of Hispanic gang members sealed off their only escape route, stepping into the alleyway with between fifteen and twenty members present. They were also armed with bats, knives, and chains. Marcus said, "We knew we were in deep shit. There was no way out without a severe and brutal fight."

They had come into Florence 13 territory unarmed, moving fast and silently in the hopes of a quick hit-and-run operation. Now they were outnumbered by armed and very pissed off and experienced Florence 13 gang members who were closing the gap and preparing to make them pay dearly for the incursion. Marcus said that he felt real fear that they may not survive the day. It was a very real possibility they could be seriously injured or killed. There would be no magical help from the police, and they could not call their own neighborhood for help. This was the 1960s—there were no cell phones or pagers; they were on their own. He said, "Just when it looked the most hopeless, Raymond ran to a nearby fence, and in one quick, violent move pulled a thick and heavy board off the fence." Marcus continued, "He yelled out to the small, desperate group 'get behind me!' Raymond then waded into the nearest group of Florence 13 gang members and began, "knocking the shit out of anyone that came close to us. When it was all over, somehow, someway, he got us all out of there, unharmed. We were in serious shit and then when we thought it was hopeless, Raymond brought us through it all uninjured. We all looked at him in a different light after that. He seemed larger than life; it was like he just could not lose."

One elder statesman of the Crips I interviewed dropped the comment I'd heard over and over again, "Here is something that no one knows." He was right. I was stunned at the tactical and logistical insight that James Ward would provide into the Crips and the way Raymond Washington had organized and made contingency plans. He said, "One day I was seeing a girl in another neighborhood. I had dressed neutral so that it was not obvious that I was not from their neighborhood. I was in enemy territory but back then if they did not know you, you could travel as a civilian and be fairly safe. As I walked up to the house, the girl's older brother came out and looked at me. He looked me up and down, and then nodded at me and continued walking away down the sidewalk. I thought I was cool. I went in the house to see the girl I was there to see. After a while I got ready to leave and looked out at my car parked in her driveway. There was her older brother and several other dudes sitting all up on my car. It was obvious I was in deep shit. I was in enemy territory, alone, and I had been made, and now they were waiting outside for me. I asked the girl if I could use her phone, and she said sure. I called one of the houses we had set up and told one of my set where I was, what the situation was, and how many enemy were present. My homie told me to sit tight, they would be on their way.

"Less than half an hour later a car rolled up. It was my set. It looked like there were only two people in the car but that was a deception. We never gave away our hand in battle. We always rolled with as many people as we could fit in the car, brothers would be laying on the floors, the seat, and hiding in the trunk so that when we got out, there were suddenly a lot more warriors there then you had counted as we drove up, and we were always armed!

"This tactic saved us more than once, not only in gang fights, but also from the cops who would be looking at a car loaded with ten to fifteen Crips, but when we passed them on the road it looked like there were only two. Anyway, that day my homies got out, and we took care of business. The set that was sitting on my car got an education in Crip tactics that day and then I got the fuck out of there." I asked Ward what neighborhood was that in, what set? He replied, "That was a set called Bonezilla, there were a lot of sets around then. I don't know if they are still around, most of them got gobbled up into the Crip nation. Lots of people talk about sets that held their own against the Crips—at first it wasn't like that, people don't realize a lot of the Blood sets were Crips at first, and then switched later."

I asked Ward what he meant when he'd said that he called one of the houses they had set up. Ward replied, "This is something that no one knows from outside the set. We had houses set up that always had someone present. Phone numbers were assigned to each house and someone was always there. It was a place that we could hang out, lift weights, or regroup after a battle, they could be a place to re-arm or gather ammo if we needed to regroup. No one outside the gang knew where they were, or who the house belonged to. They would belong to people in the neighborhoods sympathetic to our cause. So if you got into some shit, you called a number and there would be backup rolling your way on a mission in minutes. I know that no one has ever told you that! It was a well-guarded secret. Raymond had set up these "clubhouses" early on as places to hang out with our people, our set. We could meet girls or lift weights or just hang out if things got bad at home. Either way they were all over the city and no one knew, not our enemies, and not the cops. The houses would be used to keep stashes of weapons and ammo. That way if an emergency occurred, the gang would have many places to go to and arm up. If the cops hit one house on a raid and seized the weapons there, the gang would not be left without arms and ammo."

I was stunned at the obvious practicality of this. Again, these were military-like tactics employed by Raymond, who had absolutely no military training at all. These "safe houses" were established after the gang had been growing for a while and spoke a lot to the span of control, coordination, and planning that went into the Crips' organization behind the scenes. It reminded me of the stories about the Black Panther clubhouse that Raymond and his brothers would go to every morning for protection and breakfast. The idea had evolved to another level with the formation and growth of the Crips.

Later, as I rode through the neighborhoods with Raymond's younger brother, Derard Barton, while he pointed out where Raymond had lived and where Craig Craddock had lived, he mentioned, "That house right there was an ammo dump," as we passed a non-descript brown house with a flat roof and red ceramic tiles over the porch awning on the left-hand side of the road at 747 East 77th Street. I asked what he meant, leaving nothing to chance. He looked at me impatiently, like I was a complete dumb-ass, and said, "Ammo dump! You know, we kept weapons there and guns." He was confirming what Ward had told me. There were in fact individual locations to house the Crip sets weapons and ammo for battle.

Another insight into the organizational skills, and understanding of human psychology that Raymond Washington possessed, came in an offhand remark that Derard Barton made while we were looking at old pictures of Raymond Washington and the Crips. I asked if Derard knew the names of any of the gang members in one particular photo that showed Raymond accompanied by three other men. He replied, "The only one I know is 'Fast Black.' He was the spokesperson for the Crips." I asked what he meant to make sure I had heard him correctly; to be honest I thought I must have misunderstood. Again, frustrated with my obvious stupidity, he said, "He was the spokesperson, the media rep. Whenever the media wanted to speak with a Crip and Raymond got word of it, he sent Fast Black. Raymond wanted nothing to do with the media. He hated that kind of attention and did not want them to know who he was, or that he was the leader of the Crips."

I was stunned. Raymond realized that everyone in the organization had different skill sets to offer, and made the most of their potential. Again, real insight into the exceptional leader he was, and how he was able to motivate and mobilize so many of the youth in Los Angeles to join the Crips. The Crips had a media representative, who knew? Derard continued, "I remember one time there was a media event and they had requested someone to show up to represent the Crips. Raymond sent Fast Black, and I asked him why. Raymond replied, 'Gates will be there, and I don't trust that he won't arrest everyone that shows up for anything that they can get on them. I told Fast Black to go rep us and let him know what to expect.'"

Ward told me another incident that showed the benefit of what he called "the Crip training centers." He said, "One day three brothers were at a theater and got hemmed up by another set. They were in trouble, outnumbered, and had no escape. So they made the call. We rallied the troops and loaded up in the cars, packing as many in each car as we could. When we rolled up on the theater it looked like there were four of us and the other set was cocky, then we started piling out and gave them a beat down. The Crips preferred to fight with fists and maybe a knife or a bat." He continued, "What would be the point of all that lifting and training to learn to fight if you did not use it and prove yourself? I mean we had guns, there were always guns, I won't lie, but we preferred to go toes, and test our skills instead of shooting some fool."

Ward also made the comment that, "As the police shut down the Black Panthers and started to put their members into jail their influence on the younger generation coming up under Raymond was felt a lot less. The younger generation had no idea of the Black Panthers' influence and the ideas they had tried to instill in the community. So all the younger Crips were about was money. The Original Crips that came up on the East side were heavily influenced by the Black Panthers. Their message was about black pride, being strong, having unity and respecting the elderly, and our women and the neighborhood. That is what separated us from the West side, the Black Panthers' influence and ideology."

John McDaniels recalled the first time, "We rolled in a stolen car. Like I told Tony Craddock yesterday, you never rolled in a stolen car. Me and my younger brother, Curtis, we did; Curtis went everywhere Craig and I did. We did everything together." McDaniels said his brother was shot and killed, and his killer is currently locked up. He is about to get out and people are looking for him already.

"Man, when I was fifteen-years-old, I had to fight Bunchy Carters' brother, Kenny Carter. He came up to Fremont and was robbing everyone. He tried to rob me, and I wasn't having none of that. I knocked his ass back. Now he is in the pen, and he is BGF; he was Crip but now he is BGF. That same day after school there were about one hundred dudes waiting for me and Raymond after school. I had to fight Robert Munsey (Big Munsey) and we went about three rounds before it got broken up. The teachers broke up the fight. They all carried guns and they let us know; they showed them to us to let us know they meant business and not to fuck with them.

"Anyway, man, back to the stolen car story, Raymond got caught by the police racing it in the big alley. His cousin, Sammy Spillman, showed up one day when we were in junior high school, driving a '63 Impala. I asked him whose car is that? He said it was his aunt's. So I jumped in and Craig Craddock jumped in the front seat and Craig said, 'Hey, man, stop in the liquor store at 78th and Central.' So we did and went in and got chips and a soda, you know we wasn't much older than thirteen. When we got back in, I saw that Sammy started the car with a fingernail file. I said to myself, goddamn, this motherfucker has us in a stolen car! We got to 74th and Wadsworth, and I told them to let me out by that fireplug and they did. Later on that day, they gave the car to Raymond, and he took the car to the big alley and started racing. He drove like a fool! He was crazy. He started doing hook slides and donuts and racing, then the police caught him, and he got hemmed up. We found out later Sammy got the car from USC."

RAYMOND AS A MENTOR/LEADER/LEADERSHIP STYLE

Raymond Washington's leadership style was very situationally oriented. Reading through these accounts I can see examples of each of the six recognized styles of leadership as discussed in the article "Leadership Style" in *The Wall Street Journal*.[51]

This is not remarkable by itself, but remember that he started the Crips between the ages of fifteen and sixteen, with bare minimum education, and absolutely no management or leadership training. He just understood leadership at a gut level and perfected his skills by trial and error. He called meetings of the Crips (democratic), demanded unflinching toughness and heart in the face of adversity (pacesetting), and when necessary he took control of an incident in an emergency (commanding). There are also accounts of mentoring (coaching) and of Raymond discussing the direction the Crips were headed (visionary). Keep this in mind as you read the accounts of the life of Raymond Washington. There are many levels to each of these stories.

Derard stopped for a moment and started to become emotional as he recalled this next story. He said that everywhere Raymond went in the city, whether it be Compton or Watts, the East side of Los Angeles or the West, he would get out of the car he was driving, and once the neighborhood Crips recognized him they would come running up to him and call out, "Raymond, Raymond, our righteous leader!" (See Pics 5-1, 5-2) Raymond would shake hands with his fellow gang members and ask how they were? Was there anything they needed in their neighborhood? He would spend some time talking to them and sharing stories about battles they had fought with rival gangs, make plans on retaliation, and then leave to the next neighborhood. Derard said, "It was like that everywhere he went. The people worshiped him and loved him."

This account struck me as very interesting for a couple of reasons. First, military commanders use this very same tactic worldwide. Troop commanders will visit troops in the field and do "health and welfare" visits. It helps them to establish a face-to-face relationship with their troops and to hear firsthand how things are in the field. They find out what is needed, and how the battles are progressing from a foot soldier's point of view. It is standard practice in the military today. Raymond Washington knew the value of the practice and did it intuitively. He had never served a day in the military. Additionally, it was surprising to hear the way the rank-and-file gang members referred to him as their "righteous leader." I first found this to be a little unbelievable. I assumed it was just Derard's own hero worship of his older brother coming out in the story, and was greatly embellished. Later, after conducting several more interviews, talking to Crips who were there at the beginning, I heard this same exact comment over and over. They actually referred to Raymond as their righteous leader, and worshiped him with a religious fervor that reminded me of the way people viewed John F. Kennedy after his assassination. The emotions that people felt then about Raymond, and surprisingly still feel today, were very apparent as I interviewed gang member after gang member.

Raphael Pattaway's account of another incident further detailed Raymond's role as a mentor and mediator in the neighborhood. He said, "One thing that Raymond always used to teach us was there are always two sides to every story and to never jump to conclusions. He would hear one side of the story and then he would go find out the other side for sure. He never took anyone's word as the whole story. He was a thinker, he didn't just act, he thought things through.

"Another time, some younger guys had got into it with some older guys from Watts. The older guys had come into our neighborhood and were talking trash. The two groups did not know each other, and they were having some words. The younger guys were in a car and the older guys were thinking they were gonna bully them. The younger guys had guns and were getting ready to kill the older guys for talking trash in their neighborhood. Raymond stepped in and diffused it. He told the older guys, 'Don't come talking crazy in this neighborhood, these younger guys will kill you! These young cats is my homies too!'"

Tony Craddock recalled the split with the Avenues set much the same as Derard. However, he added, "Around 1971 we was going to the Watts festival. There was a festival every year on the anniversary of the Watts riots, and Raymond showed up at the Watts festival. I tell you what, if that niggah didn't have one hundred fifty to two hundred motherfuckers following him, then he did not have one. (See Pic 3-3) Everyone wanted to be a Crip! I don't know if it was his personality or charisma or what the fuck, but I swear to god he had at least two hundred Crips show up with his ass that day. They were all wearing overalls and no shirt, and you could tell who was who." This event occurred just two years after the founding of the Crips, and spoke strongly to the nerve that Raymond had stuck in the city's urban culture with the subculture of the Crips and the message he had built into its structure.

James Ward told me of one neighborhood visit that Raymond made. He said, "Raymond pulled up and got out of the car and leaned back against it, waiting. (See Pic 5-6) We walked up to him getting ready to hit him up and challenge him, asking where he was from and why the fuck he was in our hood and then we recognized him. It was Raymond Washington. We called out to everyone in the neighborhood that Raymond Washington was in the hood and walked up to him, touching his arms and calling out, 'Raymond, Raymond, our righteous leader.'" Ward said that Raymond would stop and talk to them, asking how they were, making sure to speak with each and every one of the Crips present, and then always he left some tactical advice. Over and over he would tell the Crips, "Never ever approach a car you don't recognize." This tactic was ingrained in them from day one.

Ward lived next door to Raymond and recalled one day that Raymond invited him to "roll with me lil man, we gonna go see some people tonight." Ward said that Raymond picked him up at night and took him from neighborhood to neighborhood throughout Los Angeles. Ward remembered they were driving Craig Craddock's orange Camaro, and they spent the entire night rolling from Inglewood to Compton, East side to West, hitting all of the neighborhoods. He said that everywhere they went, Raymond would stop and talk with Crips gang members and that as soon as Raymond was recognized, it was the same routine over and over. The neighborhood gang members would cry out as they realized it was, in fact, Raymond Washington, "Raymond, Raymond, our righteous leader is here!" Ward said that he knew on some level that Raymond was respected in the streets, but he'd had no idea how much until that night. He said he felt privileged to be riding with Raymond, and that his status in the gang grew immediately because of the nighttime visit.

The following week Raymond walked Ward to school. He said Raymond was just talking to him like he was a friend, acting like a big brother, asking him how he was doing, and if he needed anything. When Ward arrived at school, the word had spread on the streets and in the hallways of the school that he had been seen walking with Raymond Washington. Ward said, "I was an unknown, nameless kid walking the halls of the school the week before, but now I was a celebrity. I had instant respect because Raymond had taken me with him that night and then later walked with me to school. From that point on, I rolled with Raymond and I put in work trying to gain more respect for myself, the Crips, and for Raymond."

Again and again, I heard this account repeated of how Raymond was greeted in the growing Crip-controlled neighborhoods in Los Angeles. I admit it still seemed exaggerated and theatrical. Then I heard this story from Derard Barton. Sitting in my car talking about forty-year-old memories of his dead brother was difficult for Derard. For thirty-five or more years he's had to listen to his brother's name being dragged through the dirt, and misrepresented. (See Pic 4-6) Derard will be the first to tell you that Raymond was no saint. He was far from perfect, and definitely hurt a lot of people and—more likely than not—personally killed several gang members or had a hand in several deaths of rival gang members. Gang life is ugly and brutal, and Raymond Washington was at the top of the Crip Nation. He founded it, controlled it, and ran it with an iron fist. However, he was still just a man.

Derard went quiet for a moment as he started to tell me about a party Raymond had attended in Inglewood. He said, "A cousin of mine was at a house party one night in Inglewood, and after the party had been going for a couple of hours he told me that Raymond showed up and quietly stood in the doorway. A few moments passed and the party became eerily quiet. Everyone in Inglewood knew who Raymond Washington was and of his reputation. No one knew what to expect." Raymond was dressed down in typical Crip attire, looking sharp, checking the crowd to make sure that he had everyone's attention while he stood silent, waiting. Finally, seeing that he had everyone's attention at the party, he started to speak. According to Derard, he said, "I am Raymond Washington," he paused and then said, "and these are the Crips!" Raymond then held both hands just above shoulder level and snapped his fingers, one hand pointed to the left, the other to the right. Simultaneously the Crips entered the party single file on either the left or the right side of Raymond as he continued to stand in the doorway. From that point on, the party belonged to the Crips. People who were present were greeted by Stanley Williams pointing a shotgun at their heads while the Crips robbed them.

Ray Rhone was present at the party and provided an eyewitness account of the incident. He said that Williams pointed the shotgun at him until Raymond recognized him. Raymond told Williams, "No, give him a pass and let him go, he is my cousin." Williams moved onto the next guy, and Rhone escaped, unharmed. This was in 1971, and the Crips were just two years old. Notice the use of guns already very present, which is in direct conflict to other reports, claiming Raymond did not want the Crips using guns.

Ray Rhone described a couple of other events that involved the Crips that I had not heard of. Rhone said that he had attended a dance at the gym in Darby Park in Inglewood, California in 1971. He said that Raymond Washington came in with his boys and again made the same theatrical entrance. He announced, "I am Raymond Washington, and these are the Crips." Rhone said, "The Crips began robbing the people at the dance." He remembered two guys there that were hardcore and tough, and who knew martial arts. They fought back against the Crips. He said, "They were holding their own and doing a pretty good job until Raymond waded in-between them and knocked them apart, then they got the hell beat out of them."

It is no wonder Raymond was worshiped by his fellow gang members with that kind of theatrical presence and status. No matter where they went, the Crips were respected or feared, or both, and it was due to his leadership, showmanship, and brutality.

Raymond not only had a reputation for being respected by the Crips, they felt safe around him, protected by him. He had survived so many battles and fights, with both fists and guns, he appeared to be omnipotent. He seemed unable to lose. On the opposite side of the street, the mere mention of Raymond Washington being involved in a dispute, fight, or being on the opposing team caused his enemies to be instantly discouraged and racked by fear. His reputation was unparalleled in modern day. The familiarity of the following story haunted me. I had read about another warrior with this kind of mythical status in battle, but I could not recall where. Eventually, quite by accident, it came to me.

In John Irwin's Book, *Lifers: Seeking Redemption in Prison*, Raymond's God-like status on the streets is mentioned in an interview with Jerry, a lifer in prison, and a Crip. Jerry described growing up on the East side of Los Angeles. "I was a close friend of Raymond and I thought of him as a 'God.'" (Page 22)

Meanwhile, being Raymond Washington's brother had some benefits and some very real hazards. Derard recalled that when people at school found out that he was Raymond Washington's younger brother, he was an instant celebrity. Other kids from his neighborhood instantly liked him. He tried to do his own thing and be his own man, but living in Raymond's shadow would forever change his life. He realized early that he had to be careful who knew about his infamous older brother. Raymond's battles for the streets resulted in casualties and enemies, people who wanted revenge, and were looking for any weak spot in Raymond's defenses. Derard was a target.

He recalled getting into a beef one day with a kid in school, and later that day Raymond asking him how school had gone. "Raymond was like that, he was always looking out for everyone in the neighborhood." Derard mentioned that he had a problem with another kid, but that he had it handled. Raymond nodded and did not say much. However, the next day when school let out, standing outside the school were thirty Crips led by Raymond Washington. A statement was being made. Any harm that came to Raymond's family or friends would be dealt with brutally. School security guards diffused the situation, and later Derard admitted to me that the security guards had come to him and asked that if there were any problems if the future to let them deal with it. Derard said they asked, "Please do not involve Raymond in anything that goes on here at school, let us handle it, okay? If you have a problem, you come straight to us, and we will take care of it."

James Ward remembered when he and Derard Barton and another kid named Ricky were between thirteen and fourteen, and still riding bikes. Ward had met a girl in another neighborhood, and she had invited him to come to her house to hang out. Ward said that the girl was very flirty, and he liked her a lot, so he convinced Derard and Ricky to ride with him to the nearby neighborhood. This was at a time when you never went anywhere alone. The three boys rode their bikes into the girl's neighborhood, and were caught immediately in a deadly ambush. The girl had set them up to be killed. Shots rang out as bullets angrily buzzed past their heads and ricocheted off the pavement at their feet. They turned and rode off as fast as they could, hoping to avoid being shot. A valuable lesson was learned that day. Raymond's enemies would set you up in imaginative ways, using females, promises of sex, alcohol, or drugs to lure you in and then kill you. Crippin was definitely not easy, and could be lethal if you slipped up even for a moment.

Derard also recalled he was a passenger on a Los Angeles public transit authority bus and was getting off the bus in a rival neighborhood. He said, "I was about fourteen or fifteen-years-old, and I was traveling in the city on one of those big, old buses that took people around. I got off the bus and immediately I was surrounded by a small group of rival gang members asking who I was and where I was from. I made up a name and told them I did not come from anywhere, meaning that I did not claim any gang. They did not care, and they jumped me right there. I fought back the best I could, but I was out numbered so I got beat up pretty good. Raymond was in jail for some minor offense at the time and when he got out he heard about it. He looked into it and took care of whoever it was that had beat me up."

James Ward remembered that, "Raymond was always lifting weights in the garage, and he had a lot of really nice stuff. Me and Derard set up our own gym, we got some mirrors, and had some weights. I had moved to an apartment building and there was a row of old garages in the back of the building. We had taken and set up our gym in one of those garages. One day Raymond showed up. He just had appeared; we had no idea he knew where it was. We were scared, I mean really scared. We had stolen a lot of our stuff from his gym." Ward said, "Raymond looked around and smiled, and then said to a friend that he had brought with him, 'Damn their gym is nicer than mine, ain't that a bitch!' There was no way he didn't know that the equipment we had was really his. But he never said a word. He was proud of us, and the way we had set up the gym." James also said, "And one more thing, I never even saw Raymond ever high. Lots of the other homeboys would drink and get high, never Raymond."

In the National Geographic channel's documentary, *Inside Bloods and Crips: L.A. Gangs*,[52] Raymond "Danifu" Cook described Raymond like this: "If you were with Raymond, you were with the one who could protect everybody. He liked to fight, and challenged anyone, anywhere, all the time, and he could have knocked out Tyson anytime he wanted." He continued to describe Raymond as the Brigadier General of Los Angeles. He said, "Raymond was trying to teach the gang members morals and looked out for everyone. We didn't know what morals were back then, but he was trying to teach us. Raymond would have the Crip set go on missions into affluent neighborhoods to steal their possessions and bring them back into the poor neighborhoods; he was like Robin Hood. That was how I knew him." Yet another reference to the attempt to form the culture that Raymond Washington was trying to forge with the Crips using the raw materials of South Central's value system.

RAYMOND AS A BULLY

When I title this section, "Raymond as a Bully," you must remember, in the words of Marcus Jones, "At the time bullies ruled the streets, there was no other way to be and survive. There were no police to turn to for help, no one was coming to protect you. You had to make it clear 'do not fuck with me.'"

Marcus Jones had said that Raymond could be a bully at times. Jones paused while he gathered his thoughts. Finally he said, "To tell the truth, both Raymond and Craig Craddock could be bullies and incredibly vicious to their enemies." Marcus recalled watching Raymond violently pull a guy out of a car and steal it from him, "Just because he could. He would drive the car around until he wrecked it or it ran out of gas, and then just leave it. There was nothing you could do, he was Raymond Washington, if he wanted your car he took it. You could not call the cops, they would not come." Jones stopped again, and then said, "To be truthful, I saw him do the same thing with your girl. If he wanted your girl, he took her. There wasn't shit you, she, or anyone could do about it. I guess I would call it rape, but what could you do? Like I said, Raymond and Craig could be vicious if they did not like you. Fortunately for me they liked me, and I tried hard to keep it that way."

In direct contrast, during my interview with Raphael Pattaway, he said, "Raymond had a good side, and people portray him as a crazy man. He wasn't. If he had to go to war with someone he would, and you would regret it. I mean, that was why he was the person he was. He had a reputation on the streets for a reason, but he had a good side too, and no one tells that side of him."

PHOTO GALLERY IV
FAMILY PHOTOS

Pic 4-1 and 4-2: Photos of Raymond's Father, Raymond, Sr.

Pic 4-3: Reggie Thompson (Crip) in 5th grade (fourth row, third from left)

Pic 4-4: High school graduation photo of Reggie Thompson (Raymond's brother nicknamed Crip)

Pic 4-5: From the left: Derard Barton, Raymond Washington, Wanda Thompson (Reggie's wife), Reggie Thompson (aka Crip), and Lil Reggie (infant)

Pic 4-6: Derard Barton (brown shirt) and Raymond Washington, mid-1970s

Pic 4-7: Violet Samuel with her five sons. Raymond Washington (bottom right) and Derard Barton (back row, middle)

Pic 4-8: Raymond at home with family and friends

Pic 4-9: Violet Samuel (Raymond's Mother) in 2014

Pic 4-10: Derard Barton (Raymond's younger brother) in 2014

THE CRIPS AND THE STREET

Pic 5-1: Raymond (center) surrounded by a group of Crips—note Stanley "Tookie" Williams in the back row on the left side, eyes closed

Pic 5-2: Raymond Washington in the middle of a group of Crips

Pic 5-3: Glen Barrett, aka Doobie (ball cap), Michael Tobin, aka Fast Black (large afro), Raymond Lee Washington, and Larry Currie Sr.

*Pic 5-4:Glen Barrett, aka Doobie (ball cap), Michael Tobin,
aka Fast Black (large afro), Raymond Lee Washington,
and Larry Currie Sr.*

Pic 5-5: Raymond Washington

Pic 5-6: Raymond Washington standing next to his low rider

*Pic 5-7: Raymond Washington's booking
photo—note the scar on his left cheek*

CHAPTER SEVEN

RAYMOND WASHINGTON KILLS YOU TWICE

While I was growing up, and even later as a cop, I remember hearing about funerals in Los Angeles that were held when a gang member had died. Almost inevitably there would be some kind of violent outbreak, and people would get into a vicious fight or a deadly shooting would erupt. I was always mystified as to why this happened. I do remember being in the briefing room at the beginning of a graveyard shift as a cop, and we were discussing the most recent of these funerals. We all wondered: What the fuck is wrong with these people? Why can't they stop fighting long enough to have a simple funeral? Derard Barton would answer that question with the following simple story about the psychological warfare that Raymond would employ on his enemies. Like I've said before, if you were a friend of Raymond Washington, there was nothing he would not do for you or to protect you. If you were an enemy, however, there was nothing he would not do to defeat you, even—according to this story—to the point of killing you twice.

Derard said that he had heard this story on the streets, and that Raymond had either ordered a rival gang member killed, or he had actually killed them himself. He did not know which story was true and if Raymond was involved at all. I asked if he knew who it was that Raymond was rumored to have killed. He said, "I heard that it was either Big Country or Lil Country from the Brims set." Derard recalled the version he heard: "The day of the funeral was a huge event and a lot of people attended. There were so many people there that some Crips were able to sneak in unnoticed." (Derard admits he did not know for sure if his brother was there.) This was a funeral, and no one expected anything but mourning and sadness from the family and friends of the fallen gang member. Raymond Washington was about to make a brutal point. It was not over until he said it was over.

This was a point that he made over and over in the street. *Don't even dare to cross me, and if you do, you will pay the consequences.* I don't know what the dead gang member had done to Raymond—I was never able to find out—and it probably would not really matter. This was Raymond's life day in and day out. He had chosen this life, and he lived it completely and unapologetically. The story continues that an armed man arrived at the funeral. He waited silently in line, taking his turn among the people who were there to pay their last respects, and say goodbye. As he walked up to the casket, he drew out a handgun, and shot a couple of rounds into the now desecrated chest of his dead rival. He then tipped the casket over, dumping the body out onto the floor. Chaos erupted as people dove for cover at the sounds of the gunshots, screaming and praying that another shooting and subsequent killing of family would not happen. In the chaos that ensued the gunman escaped uninjured and completely unscathed.

The legend of Raymond Washington had grown immensely in that one insanely brazen act. It was well known from that point on that Raymond Washington didn't just kill you once, he killed you twice. This urban legend was also mentioned in the documentary HBO special *Bastards of the Party*, narrated by Cle "Bone" Sloan, an Athens Park Blood member.[53] From then on, funerals of gang members would erupt in violence, there would have to be a police escort and armed security at every gang member's funeral, and still shootings would erupt, and fights would break out. The violence continues today, and has forced funeral homes to change the way they do business. The Adams Funeral Home in Compton, California has bulletproof glass as a partition and is thought to be the only drive-through funeral home in Southern California.[54]

I asked Tony Craddock if he had heard about the stories of Raymond desecrating a body at a funeral. He replied, "Raymond and Craig were always doing stupid shit like that, they would show up at an enemy's funeral, and pour blue ink all over the dead body in the casket, and then dump the body and the casket over. They would do drive-bys at the damn cemetery as the people were burying their loved ones. I am telling you, man, they was always doing stupid shit. They had no respect at all for their enemies, absolutely none."

In an article in *LA Weekly* dated December 15, 2005, neighbors described Raymond Washington as someone who protected the boys and girls from bullies from other neighborhoods, only to bully them himself. "I don't have a whole lot of good to say about Raymond," said Lorrie Griffin Moss, 48, with a laugh. She grew up directly across the street from Washington on 76th Street, just west of Wadsworth. "Raymond was a bully. A muscular bully. He wouldn't let anybody from outside our neighborhood bother us. He would bother us. Raymond could be very mean."[3]

Tony Craddock remembers, "Raymond had been picked up on a rape charge and was being held by the police. My brother, Craig, went down there to say that Raymond had been with him at the time of the rape and they asked him his name. He told them Craig Craddock and they said, 'Oh really, we are looking for you on the same charge!' They both got their asses locked up! They never did do any time on the charge. The girl that accused them was named Helen, and she had just moved into the neighborhood and was staying with her aunt. I think the thing behind it was she got caught having sex with Raymond and Craig after they had been smoking weed and drinking beer all day when her aunt came home, and she yelled rape to get out of trouble. Craig ran out the door but Raymond stayed behind because he knew he had not done anything." Tony continued, "Craig never did any time at all for anything he did."

I asked Ray Rhone if he knew of the rape charges, and what had come from them. Rhone said, "Yeah, I do remember something about that, but I don't know if it was the same incident. I remember I went to a house party one day, and Raymond was there. He asked me if I wanted some, and I said sure. He motioned to the back bedroom. I went in and there was a girl that was high on Red Devils, and they were taking turns with her pulling a gang-bang. I said no, I can't get behind nothing like this, but I heard they got in trouble over it." I asked how old Raymond was at the time, and Rhone answered, "Maybe sixteen-years-old, at the most."

CHAPTER EIGHT
RAYMOND WASHINGTON AND STANLEY WILLIAMS

A lot has been written about Stanley Williams' life, and there are few references in any of it about Raymond Washington. Most paint Raymond as a secondary figure, following Tookie's lead. Hollywood loves a good story, and from what I have read Tookie loved attention of any kind. There are several accounts in the interviews I have done with Crips gang members that were present from the beginning. Each made a point to give Tookie his due as a leader, and a Crip who was respected for his part in the gang. Every single one adamantly denied that Tookie was ever there at the beginning, and adamantly insisted that he was not a founder or a co-founder of the Crips.

For all the attention that Tookie craved, Raymond was the opposite. He preferred the quiet respect of a group of fellow gang members coming out of their houses to meet him and talk as he made his neighborhood rounds, making sure they knew he was there, and aware of their actions on the gang's behalf. He was not flashy, as Tookie was. He was quiet, confident and, as many have pointed out, he could be brutal. One Crip recalled being at a concert at the Forum at 3900 West Manchester Boulevard in Inglewood, California. The crowd was all riled up and excited to see a concert, when suddenly there was a commotion on one side of the audience. Most people assumed it was a fight, which was common at any concert. Instead, it was Stanley Williams, parading down the aisle covered in baby oil, naked to the waist, flexing and strutting around the concert aisles.

Another claim, which I was able to prove, was that Stanley Williams appeared on *The Gong Show*. *The Gong Show* was a random talent show of sorts that allowed people of various talents their fifteen seconds of fame. Often, it was a place for unknown comedians to make an appearance and get noticed. Williams appeared and showcased his talent, which was standing in-between two women in bikinis, flexing his muscular frame, again covered in baby oil, as he danced on national television.[55]

Ray Rhone said, "One of the things that I can recall is that Raymond had called a big meeting at Sportsman's Park. Now it is called Jessie Owens Park. That was where and when Tookie Williams got involved, it was 1971 or '72, and there were a lot of Crips at the park for the meeting. That was when they divided the city and made the East side and the West side. There was a shooting and everyone scattered."

The reality is Raymond and Stanley met at a record hop in Los Angeles. A record hop was a dance, informally planned, that enabled people to get together and have a good time. Raymond had expanded the Crips to Main Street, which was the original boundary separating the East side of Los Angeles from the West side. The two talked, and Raymond liked Williams. He was charismatic, and they shared a passion for fitness. Stanley had a reputation as a brawler that Raymond liked. After they spoke for a while, Raymond decided that Stanley would be his right-hand and help run the West side. The job had formerly been Melvin Hardy's. Now Williams was in charge of the West side, and Melvin was his right-hand man. It was as simple as that. Legend has it that Washington approached Williams to expand his gang to the West side of the Harbor Freeway, and Williams became the leader of the West side Crips. "It's just wrong to say Tookie was the founder of the Crips," said Wes McBride, president of the California Gang Investigators Association. Additionally, Lorrie Griffin Moss also remembers Williams coming by all the time to visit Raymond. "He'd be walking down the street looking like the Pirelli man," she said.[3]

Interestingly I spoke to one of the older Crips who told me that Williams mentioned to him one day, after he'd had a particularly intense weight lifting session, "The reason I lift so hard was just in case one day I have to face Raymond Washington in a fight. I know that Raymond is a better fighter, the only chance I can win that fight was if I can overpower Raymond."

The photo of a group of Crips taken back in the day when the Crips were under the control of Raymond and Tookie (See Pic 5-1), shows Raymond in the middle of the picture surrounded by Crips. In the back left-hand side is Stanley Williams, eyes closed, which was how he appeared in nearly every picture I have found of him. Why is Williams barely included in the picture if things were as he portrayed it in his book, *Blue Rage, Black Redemption.* In it, he says, Raymond came to him and asked if the East side could join the West. He claimed over and over that he was a co-founder of the Crips along with Raymond Washington.

BlackPast.org also repeats the claims made by Tookie that he and Raymond founded the Crips.[56] Mentioned in the article is this quote: "Alternatively, the United States Department of Justice and some social scholars claim that Raymond Washington solely founded the gang in the mid-1960s to imitate the Black Panther Party and older Los Angeles gangs." I won't even go into the validity of the book *Blue Rage, Black Redemption* point by point. Go ahead and read it if you prefer fiction.

Gangs.org also jumped on the Tookie Williams' bandwagon and listed him as the sole founder of the Crips on their website, where they state, "the street gang known as the Crips, originally founded by Stanley 'Tookie' Williams."[57]

According to Tony Craddock, "Stanley Williams was originally in a gang on the West side, and he had nothing to do with the Crips. The original West side Crips were founded by Melvin Hardy and my brother, Craig Craddock." Tony said, "Craig was on the West side so damn much that everyone thought he was from the West side, they had no idea that he was an Eastsider. Craig would spend a lot of time on the West side at record hops and stuff like that. Later on, Tookie and Jimel Barnes hooked up and claimed to be founders of the Crips, but they were never, never ever there in the beginning. What is funny to me is at the end for Tookie, Jimel even turned on Tookie and said 'Ya, he killed those people.' But what happened was Tookie had beat Jimel's ass, and he did not like that after all the times he had rubbed baby oil on Tookie so he could walk around posing and showing off. Jimel was pissed off, and Jimel turned on Tookie. Jimel was a Crip in his own right and he did his own thing. He has been shot six or seven times and lived, he was tough in his own right."

Tony Craddock also recalled, "Tookie and the Governor Arnold Schwarzenegger actually used to lift weights together and worked out together a couple of times, they were not friends but Joe Weider wanted Tookie to lift weights for him and body build professionally. But Tookie said, 'No I ain't working for no white man', being arrogant, and he was fucking with that PCP and shit. He could not see a good thing when it hit him upside the head."

CHAPTER NINE
CRAIG CRADDOCK

C raig Craddock's Mother was Dorothy Nelson and was born in Arkansas. She was twenty-nine at the time of his birth. His father was Willie Craddock. He was born in Texas, and he was thirty-five at the time of his son's birth. Craig was born in Los Angeles in the South Hoover Hospital at 5700 South Hoover Street, Los Angeles, California at 12:06 a.m. on September 22, 1954. They lived at 742 East 76th Place, Los Angeles, California. (See Pics 6-2, 8-5)

Finding any mention of Craig Craddock in Crip lore is nearly impossible. He is known to only a few of the original members, and I wondered why this was so. If he was co-founder and so critical to Raymond's success—being one of the few people that he really trusted—why is there no mention of him in any gang history? Why do noted gang historians like Alex Alonso, and LASD detectives never mention him? Everyone knows of Williams, alleged and self-proclaimed status as the founder of the Crips, but no one has heard of the real co-founder Craig Craddock, how could this be? The answer was painfully simple and obvious as I was soon to find out.

While I interviewed John McDaniels, he talked about Raymond and Craig Craddock and when they met. He mentioned that Craig had a younger brother named Tony who was near the same age as Derard. Both Derard and McDaniels agreed that the two founders of the Crips made it absolutely clear that they did not want their younger siblings involved in the set. They did everything they could to discourage their membership, and Derard said that Raymond made it clear that if he caught him having anything to do with the lifestyle or the gang he would beat his ass. McDaniels also said that, "You would never see Tony rolling through the hood if Craig was around. Craig would not let him be involved in anything he did that involved the gang." Obviously both of them knew that the course they had set on when they formed the Crips was a dangerous and deadly one and would more than likely result in a violent and premature death. For Craig Craddock that death would come a mere three years after the Crips were formed and had begun to flourish.

Craig had a job as a custodian at the Merideth Manufacturing Company, and had been working there for about a year on the night of October 5, 1972. He had dropped out of high school and devoted himself full time to the advancement of the Crips. Almost three years to the day after the Crips were formed, Craig stopped in the liquor store at 78th and Central Avenue to get an RC Cola. It was a place he frequently stopped into on his way home, and according to Marcus Jones, he saw Craig there often. Marcus Jones was home the evening of October 5th, and he is the closest thing I could find to an eyewitness account to the events that were about to unfold. He would also be able to provide some real insight into why events happened the way they did.

Marcus said, "Craig liked to stop in the liquor store there at 78th and Central late at night and get an RC. He drove an orange Chevy Camaro and everyone knew it was his. Craig and I always got along really well, but he could be vicious if he did not like you. Like, I mean, really mean and vicious and degrading. There was a guy he tormented constantly that also frequented the store. Craig would rob him of his money, and then spit in his face. Basically he did whatever he could to degrade the guy and humiliate him. I tried to talk to Craig and reason with him that he should not be treating the guy that way, but he would not listen. He said that the guy was a bitch and that he could do whatever he wanted, and the guy would never step up and face him. I told him I don't know about that—I believe in karma and you are gonna reap what you sow."

Marcus said Craig ignored him, and he did not pursue it further. He told me that he felt like he had said enough, and he did not want Craig to start in on him. I got the impression Marcus was always walking a tightrope with Raymond and Craig, trying to stay on their good side and not end up in the shitstorm of finding yourself on their bad side. Marcus continued, "Late one night I was sitting at home. We lived just four houses down from the liquor store I mentioned. I heard a couple of gunshots ring out and jumped up to look out the window to see what was going on. I looked toward the liquor store and there was Craig's orange Camaro, pulled up to the curb, the door still open, and no one inside. I ran to the store to see what happened, and there was Craig lying on the sidewalk. He had been shot twice in the chest, and was taking his dying breaths. Blood gurgled out of his chest and mouth, as he gasped for air." Marcus found out that Craig had gotten out of the car to get his nightly RC Cola and that the guy he continually tormented was waiting for him. Marcus said, "The guy's name was Steve. Steve had enough of Craig's shit and came at him with a handgun. He told Craig you had better leave me the fuck alone, or I will kill you! Craig spit in his face, and Steve had enough. He shot him twice in the chest and dropped him right there. I watched my friend die, and he died for nothing; he just did not know when enough was enough."(See Pic 6-5)

According to Derard, Craig had a girlfriend named Clairette, and she was present when the murder occurred. Derard had heard that she and Craig had been coming back from a drive-in movie, and they stopped in the liquor store. There was a guy there that Craig had bullied and taken money from and humiliated on a regular basis, and they had words and the guy shot Craig right there in front of her. I was never able to verify that with her or locate her. She is pictured in one photo I have of Raymond Washington sitting on the couch, wearing a brown leather jacket. (See Pic 3-4)

When I interviewed John McDaniels, he confirmed the account that Marcus Jones had given as the truth of the story about how Craig Craddock had died. He said, "The night Craig died, it hit Raymond hard. I can still remember the exact date, October 5, 1972. Raymond was angry like I had never seen him before. We gathered up in a car and went looking for the guy that had killed Craig. At first we could not find him, but Raymond had it set in his mind that there would be a price to pay for his friend's death and it would be immediate, it would be tonight. We were armed and there was no doubt what Raymond intended to do. After a while, I thought it over and realized I did not want any part of what was about to go down."

McDaniels said, "Have you seen *Boyz N The Hood*?" I said I had. He replied, "Well that scene where they go out looking to kill Doughboy's brother's killers was very similar to where we were at that night. I was Cuba Gooding, Jr. that night. I told Raymond to stop the car where we were, and he did. I said I was getting out, and he said 'okay.' He never held it against me, but it did not stop him from continuing to search for Craig's killer. I walked home that night through the streets, alone, quietly wondering what would happen. The next day I heard that they had finally found who they thought had killed Craig Craddock and killed him, later though we found out they killed the wrong guy. The guy they killed had not killed Craig Craddock."

McDaniels sat silently in my car looking out the window as he remembered that night, and Derard was quiet as well. These are powerful, emotional memories for these aged street warriors, looking back on the deeds they witnessed or participated in as younger, more rash, and inexperienced men. Remembering them now, through the eyes of older and wiser adults in their fifties and sixties was not easy. The car was quiet for some time before they continued talking. McDaniels said, "So that is why no one has heard of Craig Craddock. He died early in the history of the Crips, and if I remember correctly, he was the first of the original East side Crips to die in the streets of Los Angeles." Craig Craddock died fourteen days after his eighteenth birthday. (See Pic 8-6)

I also spoke to Tony Craddock about his older brother, and he had some very interesting insight into Craig and Raymond Washington.

The first point that Tony wanted to make was that his brother was very smart. He said, "Craig was always getting the grades in school. He did very well in science and math." I asked how he got so off track. He replied, "It was his skin! Craig was very light skinned; he had blue eyes and light skin, and light brown hair. It caused him a lot of problems in school. The darker skinned blacks would call him a white boy and torment him. I remember the day that one of the counselors from Edison Junior High School called and told my mother that Craig was hanging around some shady characters at school. She described them to my mother as all wearing black leather coats, and walking with canes through the hallway. The counselor was worried about her son, Craig, but by then it was too late."

According to his younger brother, "Craig was always scheming, conniving, and plotting. He was stealing money at an early age and had no problem taking your shit, no matter who you were." Tony recalled that his mother had found out that Craig had been forging checks from her account and cashing them at a nearby market. His mother and the grocer had worked out a deal where Craig would go to the store to buy her things and pay with a check. "It wasn't too long before Craig had started forging his mother's checks and getting cash out of his mother's account. It was never in large amounts, five dollars here, eight dollars there, and it took some time before she figured it out." Craig was between eleven and twelve-years-old.

Craig, like Raymond, was always watching gangster movies and liked to emulate the movies to the maximum. Tony said, "Here is an example for you: our dad had a pool table in the recreation room of our house. We played there a lot, and I had a group of friends over playing pool one day. Craig came into the room and started to rob us. I was like no, fuck that! We aren't giving you our shit! Craig pulled out a revolver and shot one round into the ceiling, and said 'all right now motherfuckers, I ain't playing, give me your shit!' I could not believe it! I will be damned if that niggah didn't come back there and rob all of us, me included!"

Tony said, "You will hear a lot about Craig being Raymond's right-hand man, it was not like that. Raymond was the brawn, he loved to fight, and when I say he loved to fight, I mean he really loved it! But my brother, Craig, he was the brains. He would always be scheming about how to get to you, watching you, and thinking of what he could do to separate you from your money, wallet, or car. It was Craig that turned Raymond onto robbing people." Marcus Jones' interviews conflicted with this version of events. He remembered Raymond robbing other kids at an early age in front of the White Front sporting goods store. Tony said, "Yeah, if you saw these two niggahs walking down the street coming at you, you would be wise to step aside, cuz they were always up to no good. Those two were a pair, a nightmare walking! Them niggahs was chaos and mayhem, and they was always up to no damn good."

I was laughing hard at this description, and I have to admit I appreciated Tony's brutal honesty, and I liked him immediately. I asked him about the night that Craig died and what he knew about it. He said, "My brother, Craig, never did know when to let up, he was always fucking with people and trying to intimidate them. He had been fucking with this guy named Steve for some time, robbing him, kicking him in the ass, and bullying him. The night that he died, Craig had been to a drive-in movie with his girlfriend, Clairette. They went to see the movie *Super Fly*, and when the movie was over they stopped in the liquor store at 78th and Central Avenue. Steve was there waiting. What Craig did not know was that Steve had been beat out of some money in a dice game by the McCoy boys earlier that night, and he went to get a gun. He was waiting there at the store. He had been taking Red Devils,[58] hoping to catch up with the guys that had robbed him. When Craig approached Steve, he said, 'Don't fuck with me, Craig, I got a gun, I will shoot you!' Craig did not care, he slapped Steve, or spit on him, I am not sure. So Steve shot him. He shot Craig six times and dropped him right there. Steve got into his truck and left, he went straight to the police station and turned himself in." (In reality Craig was shot twice as is verified by his death certificate.)

I told Tony that I had read in *Allhood Publications* that Craig Craddock's family believed he had died at the hands of the Los Angeles Police Department (2008). Tony exclaimed, "What the fuck are you talking about? No! No! No! My brother had done so much damn dirt out there in the streets that when he died, my father had to go to the police station and ask them to guard the viewing and prevent them from turning over the casket. Listen, he and Raymond had gone to funerals and shot up the motherfucking cemetery and shit. Lemme tell you something them niggahs was some dirty motherfuckers, man. They would do some shit that would make you stop and say, Mmm, Mmm, Mmm." At this point in the interview I burst out laughing again.

He continued, "These motherfuckers had been watching gangster flicks and shit, and it was true they would shoot you laying in the casket and then dump the body out on the floor. My brother had a cane he had made out of a broken pool cue my father had in the recreation room, and lemme tell you something. He would take that cane out and let motherfuckers know what time it was! I mean, he would knock the shit out of you with that cane in a minute. My brother was 6'4", and mean. He loved to intimidate people. There was a dude that one of my partners brought over to play pool one night. He was from the West side and when he found out who my brother was he said, 'The first time I met your brother, he beat the hell out of me for no damn good reason.' Do you know I apologized to him for my brother! It was just kind of who he was. He and Raymond knew how to work a crowd."

I read the quote from the *Allhood* article and Tony continued, "Listen, there are a lot of motherfuckers out there claiming all kinds of bullshit about the Crips, Raymond, and my brother, Craig. No one in my family ever believed that LAPD had anything to do with Craig's murder, period. Craig lived a life that got his ass killed, He would intimidate and beat the shit out of people and rob them of their money. It was as simple as this: he lived by the sword that killed him. He created a path, and he walked it. Simple. We in the family knew exactly who and what Craig was. We knew who killed him and why. There were witnesses there. Clairette and Marcus Jones both were there and told us what happened, so whoever wrote that shit about LAPD killing Craig is a motherfucking liar!"

In direct contrast to Tony's account of Raymond and Craig, James Ward said, "No matter what people tell you about Raymond Washington and Craig Craddock being mean and being bullies, I never saw it. Not once. They would check you and make sure you would stand up for yourself, and you had better do it. They did not like people who would back down and take shit off of people. So they could be rough with you, and they would test you. If you stood up for yourself, they liked you. I remember that every day Craig had a different gun, I mean every day! He would say to me, 'Hey, Lil J, come over here,' and he would talk to me like a big brother and show me his latest gun and how it worked. I still have a lot of love for both of them. So, no matter what you hear about them being mean and bullies, I never ever saw it. They treated me like I was one of their own, like I was somebody that mattered."

Derard recalled that his mother tried to get Raymond to change his ways, and tried over and over to tell him that he was going down the wrong path. She recited a bible verse to Raymond during one heated argument and basically told him that he did not want to "face God" after some of the deeds he had done. Derard said that Raymond wasn't listening, and his mother continued lecturing him. Finally, Raymond had had enough, and replied, "Momma, what do you get when you spell God backwards?" They glared at each other for a few moments. At that point the argument ended.

Derard said, "Raymond could be stubborn like that but also at other times he would surprise you with an act of compassion." There was one incident in particular that stuck out in Derard's mind. "Raymond had come across some Crips that had a Blood gang member hemmed up and they were about to kill him. Raymond recognized the Blood and knew that he was seeing a girl that was a friend to one of our sister's-in-law. He told his Crips to give the Blood a pass, let him go." They could not believe what they were hearing, but Raymond was clear, "Let him go, now!" They released the Blood gang member.

One night the police came to Derard's mother's home, and knocked on the door. She answered and found the house surrounded by police officers, guns out of their holsters on all four corners of the building. They were looking for Raymond, and she was told that he was suspected of having participated in a robbery. She let them in and they searched the home thoroughly. When they were satisfied that Raymond was not home, they left. A few moments later, Raymond came in through the back door. He said, "Momma, what were the cops here for?" She told him what they had said, and asked where he had been. He told her he had been watching from a neighbor's garage as they surrounded the home, and so he just waited there for them to leave. Derard laughed about this incident as he told me how unaffected Raymond had been by the events.

While I interviewed James Ward, he also recalled the incident but from a different perspective. Ward lived next door to Raymond Washington and remembered vividly that same night when the police arrived and surrounded the house. He said that his mother was watching, and saw Raymond outside. She knew they had come for Raymond and pulled him into her home, telling him to "stay put until the police leave the neighborhood." Ward said, "She hid Raymond, protecting him from the police, putting her own family at risk. She did this because she did not trust the police, and because Raymond protected the neighborhood." Obviously she did not fear Raymond, and did not see him as a bully, and agreed with Violet Samuel and Derard Barton when they said Raymond was seen as a protector of their neighborhood. (See Pic 5-5)

Two weeks later the police were back, this time much later in the evening, and with more assets. Derard recalled, "They had officers at all four corners of the house, shotguns at the ready, watching everything. There was a helicopter flying overhead with a spotlight shining on the house. We called them Ghetto birds back then and we called the police "One Time," and we still do. The police arrested Raymond for the robbery and took him away. When we went to court and the judge read the verdict saying that Raymond was guilty, Raymond erupted. He yelled at the presiding judge, 'What the fuck are you talking about? I am not guilty! What the fuck are you talking about motherfucker?'" (See Pic 5-7)

PHOTO GALLERY VI
LANDMARKS AND PLACES OF INTEREST

Pic 6-1: Raymond Washington's childhood home

Pic 6-2: Craig Craddock's childhood home

Pic 6-3 and Pic 6-4: Apartment building that Raymond Washington was killed in front of—he was staying in apartment #8

Pic 6-5: Liquor store at 78th and Central where Craig Craddock was shot and killed two weeks after his 18th birthday

Pic 6-6 and Pic 6-7: Noteworthy streets and signs

Pic 6-8, Pic 6-9, and Pic 6-10: Noteworthy streets and signs

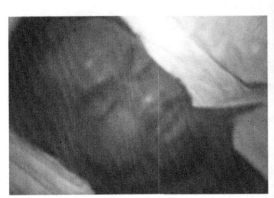

Pic 7-1: Raymond Lee Washington at his viewing

Pic 7-2: Raymond Lee Washington memorial leaflet from the funeral home

Pic 7-3: Final resting place of Raymond Lee Washington

Pic 7-4 and Pic 7-5: Final resting place of Raymond Lee Washington

Pic 7-6: Evergreen Cemetery where Craig Craddock is buried

CHAPTER TEN
THE RETURN OF ACHILLES

Reading these various accounts of the actions and thoughts of Raymond Washington, I was struck by the familiarity of the stories. I had heard accounts similar to these somewhere before, but I could not immediately recall where. It finally came to me while I was speaking with Raymond's youngest daughter, Rayshana Washington, about her father. I was struggling to describe the stories I had been told and the duality of her father. I recalled trying to find a way to describe his mythical status on the streets of Los Angeles, both as a fearsome warrior and tactician, while taking into account his failure to respect traditional cultural mores as he attended the funerals of his enemies and actually purposefully going out of his way to desecrate bodies and dumping them out of their caskets in front of their grieving families.

Then it hit me. I had read about another warrior with a similar zest for battle. He too was unable to be defeated in spite of overwhelming odds, and possessed a mythical-like status among his friends and enemies alike. He too refused to bow down to the powers that controlled his society, and lived life on his own terms by his own value system, unencumbered by loyalty to kingdoms or kings he lived for battle. He too had denied his enemies a proper burial after having killed them in battle. It was not enough to defeat his enemies; he had to belittle them and degrade them in front of their families until the fires of rage that burned in his heart had cooled, and he listened to wiser counsel. I am speaking of Achilles and the account of his battles with the armies of Troy, and the killing of Hektor as recalled in the *Iliad* by Homer.[59]

These excerpts in particular reflect the same feeling that come from the stories about Raymond Washington, told by his family and friends.

By far the richest source of our knowledge concerning Achilles' escapades is Homer's account of the Trojan War in the Iliad. *Indeed, one may reasonably argue that Achilles is the star of the piece, and Homer himself describes his story as a tale of the rage of Achilles. Early on in the poem, Odysseus, the wily king of Ithaca, is sent on a mission to find Achilles and persuade him to participate in the coming war between Greeks and Trojans. Odysseus was a formidable negotiator, and with Achilles' thirst for glory, the embassy was successful and Achilles, leaving behind his son, Neoptolemus, sailed for Troy. With him went fifty fast ships, each carrying fifty men of his own private army, the Myrmidons—fearsome fighters who had been transformed by Zeus himself and given to his son, Aiakos, King of Aegina and Father of Peleus.*

The Achaean siege of Troy lasted for ten years and during this time Achilles excelled in battle and sacked no less than twenty-three cities in the surrounding area. Early on in the conflict, the hero also ambushed the Trojan prince Troilos as he drank at a spring and sacrificed him in honor of Apollo. This was fortuitous for the Greeks, as an oracle had decreed that if the prince were killed before he reached twenty years of age, then Troy would fall. In some accounts the murder of Troilos occurred at a sanctuary of Apollo, and this may explain the archer god's fateful grudge against Achilles.

Things, then, were looking pretty good for the Greeks at this point, but their fortunes changed dramatically for the worse when Agamemnon, King of Mycenae and leader of the Greek forces, fell out with his greatest warrior and Achilles withdrew from the conflict. The quarrel started after Achilles had abducted two beauties in one of his raids—Breseis and Chryseis. Keeping the former for himself, he gave Chryseis to Agamemnon. However, Chryseis' Father, Chryses, offered a tempting ransom for the girl's safe return. Agamemnon refused and perhaps because the girl had been a priestess of Apollo, the god was displeased with the decision and sent a plague to wreak havoc amongst the Achaean camp. Agamemnon eventually relinquished his prize, but to console himself at his loss, promptly took Breseis from Achilles. Miffed at this slight and claiming he was dishonored before all of his compatriots, Achilles and his Myrmidons stormed off to their camp to sit out the rest of the war.

Without their talismanic warrior, the Achaeans' fortunes waned and the Trojans took confidence from Achilles' absence, even reaching dangerously close to the walls of the Achaean camp in their attacks and managing to start a fire amongst the Greek ships. Agamemnon offered fabulous gifts and the return of Breseis, but to no avail, and in this hour of great danger, even Achilles' great friend, Patroklos, pleaded with the hero to re-enter the fray or at least allow him to lead out the Myrmidons in battle. Achilles agreed to the latter, and giving Patroklos his armor, made his friend promise only to engage in defensive action and not pursue the Trojans back to Troy.

When the Trojans saw the armored Patroklos, they thought that Achilles had re-entered proceedings and a panic ensued. Patroklos, flushed with success, ignored his leader's advice and chased after the fleeing Trojans, even killing the Lycian Sarpedon, a son of Zeus, and reached the walls of Troy. Unfortunately for the young warrior, Apollo, protector of the Trojans, decided at that moment to intervene, and he struck the helmet and armor from his body and guided the spear of Euphorbos to strike him in the back. Patroklos was only wounded by the blow but Hektor, the Trojan prince, was at hand to deliver the final, fatal blow. A long battle then followed over possession of the body with the Achaeans, led by Menelaos and Ajax, finally managing to take the fallen Patroklos back to their camp.

When Achilles discovered the tragedy he was mad with rage; now he would fight and take terrible revenge for the death of his friend. He immediately asked his mother, Thetis, to provide new armor and she enlisted Hephaistos, the god of metallurgy, to forge for the hero the most magnificent armor ever made. Homer describes the armor in great detail; the gleaming shield depicted all manner of scenes in gold, silver, and enamel, the greaves were of shining tin, and the helmet had a crest of gold.

Achilles the man-breaker, decked out in his divine armor and still livid with rage, took to the battlefield once more and routed the enemy left, right, and center, sending a long line of Trojan heroes down to Hades. He then went after Hektor, and although Apollo tried three times to protect the prince in clouds of mist, the two finally met in single combat outside the walls of Troy. Hektor, although a great warrior himself, was no match for Achilles, who *swiftly dispatched the Trojan, and by tying him to his chariot, dragged the corpse in front of the walls of the city in full view of his grieving family and then back to the Achaean camp, a sacrilegious act, breaking all etiquette of ancient warfare.*

Priam, King of Troy, traveled in secret to his enemy's camp in order to plead with Achilles to return the body of his son so that he might receive a proper burial. After a long and moving appeal, and with a little extra counsel from Athena, Achilles finally agreed to the old king's request.

Notwithstanding these dramatic events, the war rumbled on and Achilles continued to dominate proceedings, even killing Memnon, King of the Ethiopians and nephew of Priam. However, the end was near for the great warrior. Just as his mother had feared, despite winning glory and renown, our hero was to be cut down in his prime. Once more, it was Apollo who intervened in man's affairs and directed an arrow let loose by Paris—the Trojan prince who had started the war in the first place by abducting the fair Helen. Of course, the arrow hit the only vulnerable place, the heel, and so Achilles was sent down to Hades. The hero Ajax managed to recover the body and took it back to the Achaean camp where funeral games were held in honors of the fallen warrior.[60]

Perhaps I am wrong, but to me, the similarities between the two warriors are striking and noteworthy. I am sure that Achilles' enemies were as tormented by him as the enemies of Raymond Washington. Each man created a mystical and talismanic presence around themselves, and their uncanny abilities in battle. Each left in their wake a trail of enemy bodies. Each had their own private army, and lived almost solely for the next fight. Each had a ten-year battle for the possession of a city. Each lost a best friend in the battle. Both Achilles and Raymond Washington were more interested in the glory of war, than the spoils of war. Finally, each desecrated their enemies' bodies in plain sight of their grieving loved ones, breaking with the accepted traditions of warfare and allowing a proper burial. The scholars explained Achilles super human talents as the interference of the Greek gods. In modern times, Raymond Washington had no such explanation for his talents. He was just exceptional and, like Achilles, answered to no one.

Reality was hard for me to face. Raymond could not see the Crips for what they had become, much as I could not see the Crips for what they had started out as. Over and over again, I heard from his friends and family and fellow gang members that the Crips—like every other gang in Los Angeles at the time—was formed to protect the neighborhoods. The police had abandoned the residents of South Central Los Angeles. They were actually seen as the enemy, and after I did my research, I understood why. The department and its leadership were corrupt. Even today they continue to have severe credibility issues in South Central, which is brought to light in an article written by the *Los Angeles Times* where officers tampered with in-car recording equipment to get out of being monitored.[61] This is alarming to me as a former cop, and I don't live in Los Angeles.

The Crips started out as a gang that protected its own neighborhood, then it grew. Raymond Washington sincerely believed that it was morally correct to take from those that had more and give back to the neighborhood. Every kid is told the story of Robin Hood from the time they are little. Robin Hood took from the rich and gave to the poor, and was seen as a hero to the poor. The rich, however, saw things much differently. Additionally, something that was never talked about in the Robin Hood story, was the danger that arises from robbing someone of their possessions. What no one ever tells you in the Robin Hood story is that robbing someone of their possessions really pisses them off. They get mad as hell, and fight back. So, to continue to succeed, you have to up the ante. You have to be more violent, more ruthless, and the cycle continues to grow. Imagine the Robin Hood myth, with South Central values, and that was how the Crips started out. It could not remain that way, however, as the reputation of the gang grew.

CHAPTER ELEVEN
RAYMOND GOES TO PRISON

Raymond was locked up in Tracy Correctional Facility for a couple of years for a robbery. According to an article in *Allhood Publications*, he was locked up for his part in a murder, but that is not true. Raymond was never locked up for anything more serious than the robbery.

According to an inmate, Raymond is described as likable and friendly and that he was one of the first Crips to show up at Tracy Correctional Facility. People liked him, and wanted to join the Crips.[62]

Another account is probably more accurate, and comes, again, from the pages of *Allhood Publications*. Again, quoting Raymond Cook, "Raymond was one of the nicest guys you could meet, or he could be your worst enemy. If you treated him with respect, he returned respect. He was very negotiable. But if you wanted a war, then you said the wrong thing. Raymond was always the first person in line for a fight no matter what the circumstances were. If it was the BGF (Black Guerrilla Family), the Mexican mafia or who ever else it didn't matter because he was going to be the first to get physical. The BGF gave the Crips hell in the system, but Raymond didn't have that problem. If they had a problem with Raymond then he would get right in their face. If they had a problem with anyone in his camp he was right there. He was superhuman!"

According to Larry Harrington, a former member of the BGF who is now deceased, "When Raymond hit the yard at Tracy in 1974 there was a lot of resistance from the Muslims and the BGF, but Raymond didn't care. The brothers from Northern California weren't too fond of Raymond and what he started in the streets of Los Angeles. They felt like it was against the Black movement. They wasn't feeling Raymond at all and they wanted him dead. Raymond was a cool and likable guy, he just wouldn't take no shit."

Raymond got jumped by the BGF in Tracy, and was stabbed in the altercation that took place. Raymond was reported to have gone crazy, and responded by terrorizing his adversaries. Harrington continued, "As soon as Raymond arrived at Tracy Prison there was friction between the northern and southern blacks. Raymond was a very strong leader: daring and persistent. I remember one day we were all on the softball field in Tracy and the BGF was out to get Raymond, but he didn't care. He stood there and recruited Crips right there in the yard in full view of the BGF."

One of Raymond's older brothers—Ronnie Joe Thompson—is quoted in the magazine as recalling a phone conversation he had with Raymond while he was locked up in Tracy Prison. "Raymond called home from Tracy one afternoon and said that some guys from BGF had come to his cell and told him they were going to kill him. He told me when he came out of the cell, he kicked all their asses. They were blaming Raymond for murders that were taking place, which he had nothing to do with." (*Allhood Publications*)

CHAPTER TWELVE
AFTER PRISON

Anyone who leaves the streets for more than a week or two, and then returns, finds that something has changed. The longer you are away, the more you realize the streets are as dynamic as ever and in a constant state of flux. No two days are the same. No one ever just stays on top of what is current without constant work, listening, and paying attention. When Raymond returned to the streets after a successful run in prison recruiting for the Crips, irritating the BGF and thumbing his nose at the status quo, he returned to Los Angeles and found that some things in the Crips had changed while he was gone.

Derard Barton remembers that after Raymond had been home a couple of days, and the word got out on the streets that he was in fact back, a pickup truck pulled up in front of the house. It was loaded down with Crip gang members all there to greet him. Raymond exited the house to the familiar chorus of voices calling out, "Raymond, Raymond, our righteous leader!" He immediately silenced the group and told them to meet him around the corner out of earshot of his mother.

Ever careful and watchful, always compartmentalizing his life, Raymond did not want his mother to hear the conversations they would be having about the status of the Crips. He waited a moment or two, and then told his mother he needed to go out and left the house to meet the anxious group of gang members a block away. There they caught him up on the inevitable changes that had occurred in the gang in his absence. It would take some time to reacclimatize to the street. (See Pic 4-8)

Derard remembered Raymond was in a playful mood one day and broke into a Crip walk and started doing the original dance, poppin', lockin', and throwing in a few breakdance moves. Derard said, "No, no, big brother, it ain't like that anymore. We don't Crip walk like that anymore." And then proceeded to demonstrate the new style of C-walk. Derard said, "Raymond was lost when he got out of the pen." I imagine Raymond must have felt very old that day. He had only been gone a couple of years and already the styles and actions of the Crips had evolved. (See Pic 4-6)

Raymond was crazy according to Ray Rhone, even after he got out of prison. He had picked him up and was giving him a ride to the apartment he was staying at located at 6326 South San Pedro Street. As they were driving, he told Rhone to get over into another lane, and as they passed a girl riding a bike, "Raymond leaned out of the car and grabbed her ass." Rhone said, "He was crazy like that."

While Raymond was in prison and pressing his recruitment of the Crips, he was contacted by former professional football legend Rosie Grier.[63] Grier was spearheading a program to provide prison inmates with jobs in an attempt to help lower the rate of recidivism in the California correctional system. According to Raymond's Mother, Violet Samuel, "Rosie Grier loved Raymond and visited him often while he was in prison. Raymond later exited prison and immediately had a job at RCA thanks to Rosie Grier, but lost it when he was picked up by the police." Derard Barton said that, "Almost immediately as Raymond got out of prison, LAPD was on him, and charged him with a robbery. He was locked up for a couple of days and when it was finally shown he had nothing to do with the robbery, they let him go, but he had lost the job."

Soon after this, Violet moved to Texas to take care of her aging mother. Raymond moved with her, helping her pack and unpack. He stayed in Texas for a few months and, according to Violet, "Raymond was doing real good in Texas, but people kept calling him from Los Angeles and trying to get him to come back there. I don't know who they were, but I could tell from the phone conversations people were trying to get him to come back there."

Sometime between April and September of 1977, Raymond did return to Los Angeles and was able to secure a job through the federal employment program CETA.[64]

He was on the job for a brief period of time when he was recommended for promotion and given a supervisory position. (See Pics 8-20 through 8-23) He was working for the City of Los Angeles and collecting a check from the same government agency that employed LAPD Police Chief Darrel Gates. I wonder how Gates would have felt had he known the founder and leader of the Crips gang of Los Angeles was collecting a paycheck from the same city he was employed with. I laughed when I read the letter recommending Raymond's promotion, and realized the irony of the fact that Darrel Gates and Raymond Washington were both on the same payroll.

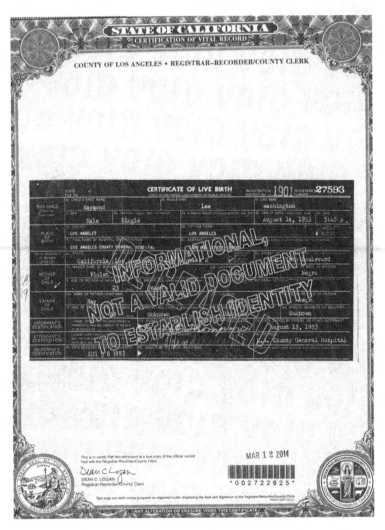

Pic 8-1: Certificate of Live Birth for Raymond Lee Washington

Pic 8-2: Original Notification of Birth Registration for Raymond Lee Washington

Pic 8-3: Certificate of Live Birth for Raymond Lee Washington
(Enlarged to show text)

COUNTY OF LOS ANGELES • REGISTRAR–RECORDER/COUNTY CLERK

CERTIFICATE OF DEATH
STATE OF CALIFORNIA

0190-036501

1A. NAME OF DECEDENT—FIRST	1B. MIDDLE	1C. LAST	2A. DATE OF DEATH	2B. HOUR
Raymond	Lee	Washington	AUGUST 9, 1979	2346

4. RACE	5. ETHNICITY	6. DATE OF BIRTH	7. AGE
Male Black	Afro-American	8/14/53	25 YEARS

8. BIRTHPLACE OF DECEDENT: Los Angeles USA
9. NAME AND BIRTHPLACE OF FATHER: Raymond Washington Sr L.A.
10. BIRTH NAME AND BIRTHPLACE OF MOTHER: Violet Samuel Tex

12. SOCIAL SECURITY NUMBER: 549-90-2416
13. MARITAL STATUS: Single
14. NAME OF SURVIVING SPOUSE: None

15. PRIMARY OCCUPATION: Garden Caretaker
16. NUMBER OF YEARS THIS OCCUPATION: 1
17. EMPLOYER: C TA-USC
18. KIND OF INDUSTRY OR BUSINESS: Federal

USUAL RESIDENCE
19A. USUAL RESIDENCE—STREET ADDRESS: 4215 W. 58 Pl., LA Calif.
19C. CITY OR TOWN: Los Angeles
19D. COUNTY: Los Angeles
19E. STATE: Calif.

PLACE OF DEATH
21A. PLACE OF DEATH: MORNINGSIDE HOSPITAL
21B. COUNTY: LOS ANGELES
21C. STREET ADDRESS: 8711 SOUTH HARVARD BLVD. LOS ANGELES
4215 Violet... Los Angeles, CA

CAUSE OF DEATH
22. DEATH WAS CAUSED BY: IMMEDIATE CAUSE (A) GUNSHOT WOUND OF ABDOMEN
24. WAS DEATH REPORTED TO CORONER: 79-9932
25. WAS BIOPSY PERFORMED: NO
26. WAS AUTOPSY PERFORMED: YES

23. OTHER CONDITIONS CONTRIBUTING: NO

INJURY INFORMATION
29. SPECIFY ACCIDENT: HOMICIDE
31. INJURY AT WORK: SIDEWALK NO
32A. DATE OF INJURY: AUGUST 9, 1979
32B. HOUR: 2220

CORONER'S USE ONLY
33. STREET ADDRESS: 6326 S. SAN PEDRO, LOS ANGELES
34. DESCRIBE HOW INJURY OCCURRED: AS ABOVE.
THOMAS T. NOGUCHI, M.D., CORONER
35C. DATE SIGNED: DEC 13-79

36. DISPOSITION: Burial
37. DATE: August 16, 1979
38. NAME AND ADDRESS OF CEMETERY OR CREMATORY: Lincoln Cemetary - Compton
39. EMBALMER'S LICENSE: 6889 Charles Stewart

40. NAME OF FUNERAL DIRECTOR: Houston's Mortuary
41. LOCAL REGISTRAR
42. DATE ACCEPTED BY LOCAL REGISTRAR: AUG 1 5 1979

STATE REGISTRAR
VS-11 (9-78)

Pic 8-4: Certificate of Death for Raymond Lee Washington

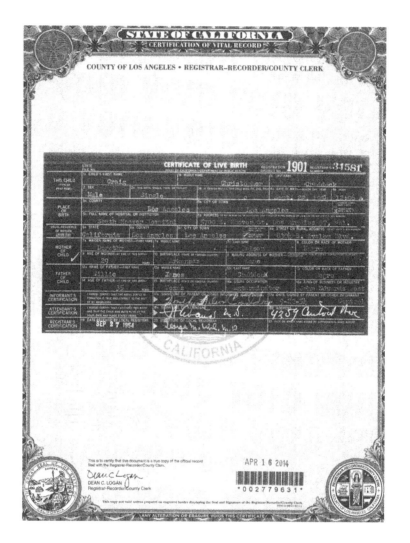

Pic 8-5: Certificate of Live Birth for Craig Craddock

STATE OF CALIFORNIA
CERTIFICATION OF VITAL RECORD

COUNTY OF LOS ANGELES • REGISTRAR–RECORDER/COUNTY CLERK

CERTIFICATE OF DEATH
STATE OF CALIFORNIA—DEPARTMENT OF PUBLIC HEALTH
7097-040763

DECEDENT PERSONAL DATA
- NAME OF DECEASED—FIRST NAME: CRAIG | MIDDLE NAME: CHRISTOPHER | LAST NAME: CRADDOCK
- DATE OF DEATH: OCT. 5, 1972 | HOUR: 232 P.M.
- SEX: MALE | COLOR OR RACE: NEGRO | BIRTHPLACE: CALIFORNIA | DATE OF BIRTH: SEPT. 22, 1954 | AGE: 18 YEARS
- NAME AND BIRTHPLACE OF FATHER: WILLIE J. CRADDOCK — TEXAS
- MAIDEN NAME AND BIRTHPLACE OF MOTHER: DOROTHY NELSON — ARKANSAS
- CITIZEN OF WHAT COUNTRY: USA | SOCIAL SECURITY NUMBER: 550-98-7126 | MARRIED, NEVER MARRIED, WIDOWED: NEVER MARRIED | NAME OF SURVIVING SPOUSE:
- LAST OCCUPATION: JANITOR | 1yr. | NAME OF LAST EMPLOYING COMPANY OR FIRM: MERIDETH MFG. CO. | KIND OF INDUSTRY OR BUSINESS:

PLACE OF DEATH
- PLACE OF DEATH—NAME OF HOSPITAL OR OTHER IN-PATIENT FACILITY | STREET ADDRESS: 78th & Central Ave. | INSIDE CITY CORPORATE LIMITS: YES
- CITY OR TOWN: LOS ANGELES | COUNTY: LOS ANGELES | 18 | 18

USUAL RESIDENCE
- USUAL RESIDENCE—STREET ADDRESS: 742 East 76th Place | INSIDE CITY CORPORATE LIMITS: Yes | NAME AND MAILING ADDRESS OF INFORMANT: MR. WILLIE J. CRADDOCK, 742 East 76th Place
- CITY OR TOWN: LOS ANGELES | COUNTY: LOS ANGELES | STATE: CALIFORNIA | LOS ANGELES, CALIF.

PHYSICIAN'S OR CORONER'S CERTIFICATION
- CORONER: INVESTIGATION | DATE SIGNED: 10-10-72
- LOS ANGELES, CALIF. 90013

FUNERAL DIRECTOR AND LOCAL REGISTRAR
- SPECIFY BURIAL | DATE: 10-11-72 | NAME OF CEMETERY OR CREMATORY: EVERGREEN CEMETERY
- EMBALMER SIGNATURE / LICENSE NUMBER L285
- NAME OF FUNERAL DIRECTOR: BARADISE MORTUARY, INC. | LOCAL REGISTRAR SIGNATURE: ... MD | OCT 11 1972

CAUSE OF DEATH
- PART I. DEATH WAS CAUSED BY:
  - (A) IMMEDIATE CAUSE: HEMORRHAGE
  - (B) DUE TO: GUNSHOT WOUNDS (2) OF CHEST
  - (C)
- PART II. OTHER SIGNIFICANT CONDITIONS:
- WAS OPERATION PERFORMED: NO | WAS AUTOPSY: YES | YES

INJURY INFORMATION
- SPECIFY ACCIDENT, SUICIDE OR HOMICIDE: HOMICIDE | PLACE OF INJURY: STREET | INJURY AT WORK: NO | DATE OF INJURY: 10-5-72 | HOUR: 2:39 P.M.
- PLACE OF INJURY: 87TH & CENTRAL AVE, LOS ANGELES | 0 MILES | NO | NO
- DESCRIBE HOW INJURY OCCURRED: AS ABOVE BY UNKNOWN PERSON

STATE REGISTRAR

Pic 8-6: Certificate of Death for Craig Craddock

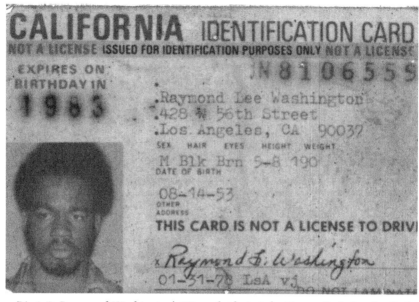

Pic 8-7: Raymond Washington's ID card, photo take 11 months before he died

BAIL RECEIPT &/or NOTICE TO APPEAR	COURT JURISDICTION ☒LOCAL ☐FOREIGN	CHECK ONE: ☐SURETY ☒☒☒ ☐BOND ☐WRIT ☒☒☒		DATE & TIME RECE 11/10/78 00T	
BOOKING NUMBER 5021170	ARRESTEE'S NAME (Last, first, middle) WASHINGTON, Raymond Lee		LOC. CONFINED JAIL	LOC.BAIL POST JAIL	TOTAL CASH REC $131.00
WARRANT NUMBER &/OR CHARGE Wr/0118696/60/40508,24002,4000A,12951 AVC		BAIL $50.00	P. A. $15.50	TOTAL $65.50	
Wr/0064244/60/40508,5200VC		$50.00	$15.50	$65.50	
DEPOSITOR/BONDING AGENCY/ATTORNEY (if writ) ☒☒ Rufus James Ratway		OFFICER RECEIVING (Signature & Serial No.) 14171			
ADDRESS 428 W 56th St LA Calif 90037		BOND OR WRIT NO. CASH	SUPERVISOR APPROVING (Verify above total) LT SALLS #7569		
ARREST MADE: ☒CITY ☐COUNTY ☐(Specify) L.A. L.A. OTHER	ARRESTING OFFICER (Agency, Division/Station, Unit, Name & Serial No.) LAPD NEWT A #17298 Fuller				

Pic 8-8: Bail Receipt for Raymond Washington, dated 11-10-78

Feb - 1978

PEOPLE THAT DO NOT REALLY KNOW WHAT THEY BE REALLY SAYING

PEOPLE THAT THINK AND SAY THEY REALLY KNOW HOW THE CRIPS STARTED, BUT DO THEY REALLY KNOW THE REAL REASON ON HOW THE CRIPS STARTED AND WHAT DO THEY REALLY KNOW WHAT THE CRIP STARTED FOR, AND HOW DO THEY KNOW WHEN THE CRIP STARTED.

HOW DID THEY KNOW WHEN THE CRIPS STARTED, WAS THEY A CRIP, WAS THEY WITH US WHEN WE STARTED THE CRIPS, HOW DO THEY KNOW, ARE WHO TOLD THEM WHEN THE CRIPS STARTED, I WONDER SOMETIME.

I KNOW THAT I DIDN'T TELL THEM ABOUT THE CRIPS AND WHEN WE STARTED CRIPING, BECAUSE WHO ARE THEY TO KNOW AND TELL HOW WE STARTED THE CRIPS, BECAUSE WAS THEY THERE WHEN WE STARTED OR WAS THEY A CRIP.

I KNOW THEY DIDN'T GO THOUGH THE THING WE WENT THOUGH TO START THE CRIPS, THEY WASN'T AROUND WHEN WE STARTED, SO HOW DO THEY KNOW THE REAL REALLY UP ON US. BECAUSE WE ARE REALLY WONDERING WHY PEOPLE SAY THING THAT THEY WAS'T IN..

SO HOW DO THEY KNOW THE REAL REASON UP ON US WHY PEOPLE LIE'S ABOUT THE CRIPS BECAUSE ONLY TEN'S OF US STARTED THE CRIPS, AND SOME OF THE BROTHER'S THAT WAS WITH US DO NOT REALLY KNOW THE REAL REASON BECAUSE THEY JUST WANNA TO GET INTO SOMETHING TO GET HELP.

DO THEY REALLY KNOW WHAT WE WAS ALL ABOUT WHEN WE FRIST STARTED AND WHEN WE FRIST HAD THAT FRIST MEETING, I DO WONDER RIGTH TODAY WHAT WAS IN THEY MIND'S WHEN WE FRIST HAD THAT MEETING TOGETHER'S.

BUT DO THE OTHER'S PEOPLE REALLY KNOW ABOUT US, I DON'T REALLY FEEL THAT THEY DON'T BECAUSE ALL THE THING I BEEN HEARING FROM THEM OR NOT TRUE.

BUT ONLY WHAT OTHER'S FEEL AND THING I JUST LET THEM THINKS IT UNTIL THE REAL REASON AND TRUE COME OUT..

ONLY A FEW PEOPLE CAN TELL YOU THE TRUE ON HOW THE CRIP STARTED AND HERE THE TRUE ON HOW WE REALLY STARTED AND HERE THE REASON AND WHY WE STARTED THE CRIP, AND WHAT WE STARTED FOR AND HERE'S SOME OF MY REASON WAS FOR..

WHAT I'm REALLY SAYING OR TRY TO SAY TO THE PEOPLE THING THAT

Pic 8-9: Beginning of Raymond writing the history of the Crips in his own words, dated February 1978 (front)

WHAT THEY REALLY DON'T KNOW, OR CAN I SAY WHAT THEY REALLY DON'T KNOW ABOUT, BUT THEY STILL GOING BE SAYING THINGS BECAUSE PEOPLE ALWAYS GONNA LIE ABOUT SOMETHING THEY DO NOT SINCERELY KNOW ABOUT BECAUSE WHAT THEY FEEL ON WHAT OTHER'S SAY AND THEY REALLY DON'T KNOW ABOUT IT, JUST BE SAYING THING TO START'S AND SAY TO HAVE SOMETHING TO TALK ABOUT, BECAUSE THEY REALLY DO NOT KNOW ABOUT JUST WHAT OTHER'S SAY FOR WHAT PEOPLE WANTS TO HEAR THEM SAY, BUT ITS JUST HEAR.

PEOPLE PUT US INTO ALL KIND OF THING, JUST TO GET CRIP'S INTO SOMETHING TO START BETWEEN OTHER'S THAT DO NOT KNOW BETTER THEN THEY KNOW THEYSELF'S.

BUT I KNOW THAT PEOPLE WANTS TO SAY THING ABOUT CRIP'S WHAT THEY REALLY DO NOT KNOW WHAT IS CRIP ALL ABOUT, BECAUSE WHAT DO THEY KNOW REALLY ABOUT A CRIP, WHAT DO THEY REALLY KNOW AS WHAT THE NEWPAPER SAY ABOUT US AND AS OTHER'S SAY AS WELL TOO, BECAUSE THE ONE WHO SAY IT THEY JUST HEAR OTHER PEOPLE SAY THING JUST TO TALK ABOUT SOMETHING SO OTHER'S CAN GO ON WITH THE TALKS ABOUT THE CRIP'S.

SO MANY SAY THING TO START THING WITH US TO FIND OUT, SO WE CAN BE THEY FOOL'S LIKE THEY WANTS US TO BE, AND THEY DO THING JUST TO PUT THE CRIP'S NAME INTO IT SO THE MAN CAN COME TO US TO TAKE TO JAIL.

I DO WONDER WHY PEOPLE SAY THEY THEY DO NOT KNOW ABOUT BECAUSE IF THEY REALLY KNEW WHY WE STARTED THEY WOULDN'T NEVER TRY TO MUCK TO START THING.

AND WHAT HOUR REASON FOR STARTING ONLY CRIPS FROM "69" CRIPS KNOWS HOW WE REALLY STARTED AND WHERE WE REALLY COMING FROM, AND HOW WE SEE EACH OTHER.

So PEOPLE PLEASE DO NOT SAY THING YOU DO NOT KNOW BECAUSE YOU REALLY DON'T KNOW MANY THING ABOUT US ONLY WHAT YOU FEEL ABOUT US.

THANK YOU

Pic 8-10: Beginning of Raymond writing the history of the Crips in his own words, dated February 1978 (back)

April 14-78

How ARE you doing Big BRo
FiNE I HoPE WELL I AM
doing Just FiNE So what
HAVE you BEEN doing LAtely
ARE you still woRking
I finish School up HERE
So I Should BE coming
To (Fort ord CAiLfornia) SomETime
This month I HoPE SO
How is EVERY Body doing
outHERE. did Simmie EVER
WRitE you. is WANDA out
THE Hospital yET. did
you SEE MAMA BEFoRE SHE
LEFT. I CALL PERRY yEste
day And HE Told mE
HE got His CAR Stolen
From TRADE TEch. I HuRd
THEY StARted Back gan gan
BAngin outHERE AgAin I HoPE
you aint BECAuse

Pic 8-11: Letter from Derard Barton to Raymond Washington expressing
hope that he is not getting back into gangs, dated 4-14-78 (front)

I Dont want ~~it see~~ nothing
~~no~~ To Helpen To you
so I am going To close
now so Be cool

love always
your lil Bro
Derard

I am sending you This picture
of me send me one of
you when you write Back

write Back

soon

Derard Barton

Co, A1st Bn
Ft Eustis VA 23604

Raymond Washington
428 west 56th street
Los Angeles CA

*Pic 8-12 and Pic 8-13: Letter from Derard Barton to Raymond Washington
expressing hope that he is not getting back into gangs, dated 4/14/78
(back and envelope)*

ME SAYING THIS TO YOU TO LET YOU REALLY SINCERELY KNOW WHERE I'm COMING FROM.

I FEEL AS A MAN THAT I CAN RELATE TO YOU IF YOU REALLY LET ME. OR CAN I SAY, I FEEL AS A MAN I CAN NOT RELATE TO YOU ANY MORE.

IT SEEMS LIKE EVERY TIME WE TALK, WE END UP ARGUING.

BUT I KEEP WISHING AND HOPING THAT BETTER THING WILL CHANGE BETWEEN US, AND THAT WE'LL BE ABLE TO ENJOY EACH OTHER LIKE WE USED TO, BECAUSE YOU JUST ONLY FRUSTRATED WITH MY PAST, AND YOU DO NOT LOOK AT WHAT HAPPENING ME NOW YOU STILL LOOK AT MY PAST, IF YOU'LL SEE WHATS HAPPENING WITH ME NOW I WOULD FEEL THING WOULD BE MORE BETTER NOW, AND I THINK YOU WOULD HAVE MORE BETTER FEELING NOW IF YOU WOULDN'T LOOK AT ME AS DOING YOU WRONG, PLEASE LOOK AT ME AS DOING YOU WITH LOVE SINCERE AND HAPPINESS BECAUSE THAT ALL I WANTS US TO HAVE WITH EACH OTHER AND THAT IS TOGETHERNESS WITH ONE ANOTHER, MY DEAR.

I DO NOT REALLY KNOW WHAT WRONG NOW; IT'S LIKE THESE'S SOME KIND OF A DOOR AND A GRUDGE BETWEEN US, I SINCERELY HOPE'S NOT?

I FEEL INSIDE MY HEART THAT WE ARE MEANT FOR EACH OTHER I SINCERELY HOPE WE ARE BECAUSE I TRYS MY BEST TO SHOW MY LOVE THAT I HAVE FOR YOU BECAUSE YOU ARE THE ONLY ONE YOUNG WOMEN I LOVE AND ALWAY WANTS TO HAVE TO LOVE, "I LOVE YOU SINCERELY AND SO VERY DEEP"

I CANT STOP LOVING YOU BECAUSE YOU GAVE ME SO MUCH OF YOUR LOVE SO LET STAY TOGETHER AND GIVE MORE LOVES TO EACH OTHER MORE THAN WE EVERY GAVE EACH OTHER, "GIVE ME YOUR LOVE ALWAYS AND FOREVER"

"I TRYS TO BE YOUR ALWAYS BECAUSE I LOVE YOU."

Pic 8-14: Handwritten letter from Raymond Washington (not dated) to Peewee, the Mother of his son, Lil Raymond (front)

I SINCERELY WONDER WHY, WHY SHE DONE NOT TRY TO UNDERSTAND ME ANYMORE WHY.

I JUST CAN'T SEEM TO GET ALONG WITH HER ANYMORE, BUT I TRY HARD REAL HARD TO GET OVER WITH YOU PEE WEE, WHAT REALLY WRONG?

I TRY SO HARD TO DO THINGS THAT I HOPE AND THINK WILL PLEASE YOU, BUT IT ALWAYS SEEMS TO BE THE WRONG THING, WHAT DONE YOU WANT ME TO DO TO REALLY LOVES YOU.

IT IT DOESN'T START AN ARGUMENT, IT END UP THAT YOU WON'T TALK TO ME FOR SOMETHING THAT I DON'T UNDERSTAND WHAT YOUR REASON WHY I CAN NOT TALK TO YOU FOR YOUR REASON, WHY WE CAN NOT TALK TO ONE ANOTHER, BUT ALL I CAN SAY I TRY TO DO MY BEST TO LOVE YOU, TO LET YOU SEE THAT NO ONE I MEAN NO ONE CAN LOVES YOU SINCERELY LIKE I "CAN" LOVE YOU BECAUSE I CAN LOVE YOU SO DEEPLY IF YOU LET ME COME IN TO YOUR HEART DEEPLY.

GIVE ME ONE MORE CHANCE TO LOVES YOU, LET ME SHOW YOU THAT I CAN LOVE YOU MORE THAN YOU THINK I CAN LOVE YOU LIKE BEFORE GIVE ME THAT CHANCE TO LOVE YOU THE WHY BETTER THAN BEFORE BECAUSE I WANTS TO GIVE IT TO YOU MORE THAN YOU'LL EVERY FEEL SINCERELY PEE WEE...

"IF YOU LET ME COME IN AGAIN YOU WILL SEE THAT I CAN LOVE YOU THE WHY YOU WANTS TO BE LOVED..."

Pic 8-15: Handwritten letter from Raymond Washington (not dated) to Peewee, the Mother of his son, Lil Raymond (back)

September 20, 1977

Dear Raymond

I am writing you this letter to let you know that I have heard from you. How is everyone doing fine I hope we are all doing fine, Ray Ray is trying to talk more each day, and getting bader each day. He gets into everything

In your letter you ask me to send you some pictures, when they come back I will send you some, if they come out right.

Raymond I will be glad when you come home. Because I miss you I think about you everyday wishing you were here. I have not been going anywhere, because there isn't anywhere to go. I just go to work and come home but I am off today.

Raymond I have been saving my money. When this month is over I will have ~~saved~~ saved about five hundred dollars.

Pic 8-16: Handwritten letter from Peewee to Raymond Washington when he was staying in Texas, dated 9-20-77 (front)

But Raymond I Still Want you to Send me Some money. Because that will help.

So Raymond I guess your having a good time out there, But don't you do nothing I wouldn't do Because I nat massing up on you just be glad when you came home to me and little Raymond.

Lave you Ray Ray and Peewee

PS Write back Soone

Pic 8-17: Handwritten letter from Peewee to Raymond Washington when he was staying in Texas, dated 9-20-77 (back)

June 27, 1979

Dear, Sweetheart

How are you doing fine I hope.
I am writing to tell you that
they change my mother date
again. She will be getting out
August 14. And if she work in
Furbough she will be coming home
on Nov 14, 1979. My social worker
said she going to talk to Aunt
and she if she can keep me.
And if she don't she is going
to find at place. for me to stay
But my mother will be coming home
every weekend if she got the
job. I hope she will ▪ let me
get my own apartment so I will
be with you. I want to come
and see you on July 4, 1979
because it is nothing to do around
here. Plus I want to see you
because I haven't seen you in
a long time. I hope everything

Pic 8-18: Handwritten letter from Sonja McNeal to Raymond Washington, dated
6-27-79, Mother of Raymond's third child, Lakeisha (front)

goes all right with you and
me. I I I start working Thursday
and I am going to save some
money. I hope that everything
will be going right before
Christmas. I am getting very
worried because I don't no what
going to happen. I If you
want to call me call this
number 480-9221. Because the
after number is the front desk
~~number I will see you~~
on July 4, 1979. So take care
of your self. I love you
very much.

                Love always
                your Lady
              Sonja and the
              baby.

Pic 8-19: Handwritten letter from Sonja McNeal to Raymond Washington, dated 6-27-79, Mother of Raymond's third child, Lakeisha (back)

WORK LOCATION SCHEDULE

MONDAY- MAY 15, 1978

Supervisor   Clean Alleys

Deb Acharyya
Work Location:

David Baca
Work Location: Between 10th Ave. and 9th Ave
                                  off 36th St.

George Deal
Work Location: Between 9th Ave. and 8th Ave off
                                  36th St.

Jessie Reyes
Work Location: Between 8th Ave. and 7th Ave. off
                                  36th St.

Matthew Velasquez
Work Location: Between 7th Ave. and 6th Ave. off
                                  36th St.

Raymond Washington
Work Location: Between 6th Ave. and 5th Ave. off
                                  36th St.

Darryl Fisher
Work Location: Between 5th Ave. and 4th Ave. off
                                  36th St.

These alleys are all paved. Alley between 8th ave. and 7th
ave. will require EXTRA pruning and grass trimming.

EACH WAGON WILL TAKE OUT AND RETURN THREE (3) TEAMS.

DO NOT RETURN PARTICIPANTS TO OFFICE DURING NOON HOUR.
_____

DISTRIBUTIONS

Work-Site Supervisors
J. Nelson
G. Singleton
C. Stanton
W. Graham
I. Blum

*Pic 8-20: CETA work schedules with Raymond Washington
supervising a clean-up crew, dated 5-15-78*

YOUTH COMMUNITY CONSERVATION AND IMPROVEMENT PROJECT

WORK LOCATION SCHEDULE

THURSDAY JUNE 15, 1978

SUPERVISOR   WORK LOCATION

Ed Frierson
Work Location: Alley behind 1187 W. 39th Street

Dave Baca
Work Location: 1406 W. 70th Street

Jesus Reyes
Work Location: Alley behind 2336 W. 23rd Street

Raymond Washington
Work Location: Alley behind 1124 W. 29th Street

Juan Madrid
Work Location: 1829 W. 49th Street

Darryl Fisher
Work Location: 1298 W. 37th Street

DISTRIBUTION

Worksite Supervisor
J. Nelson
G. Singleton
C. Stanton
W. Graham
I. Blum
B. Mason

Pic 8-21: CETA work schedules with Raymond Washington
supervising a clean-up crew, dated 6-15-78

PROJECT HEAVY
HUMAN EFFORTS AIMED AT VITALIZING YOUTH

January 11, 1978

Mr. Jerome O. Nelson
Job Development Center
University of Southern California
University Park, CA.

Dear Mr. Nelson:

The purpose of this letter is to relay the experiences I've had with Mr. Raymond Washington. Raymond, has been involved with us for several years and has demonstrated; ability to work with other people including his peers in a positive manner, eagerness, conscientiousness and an excellent attitude toward his work irregardless of the task at hand. Overall his progress has been tremendous throughout the program.

If you have any further questions please do not hesitate to call me at the Central phone number.

Respectfully yours,

Johnny R. Odom, Assistant Director
Anti-Vandalism

JRO:gp

Pic 8-22: CETA letter of recommendation from Johnny R. Odom, Assistant Director Anti-Vandalism, dated 1-11-1978

Robert Farrell
COUNCILMAN, 8TH DISTRICT

City Council
of the
City of Los Angeles
City Hall
90012

COMMITTEE CHAIRMAN
PUBLIC HEALTH, WELFARE
& ENVIRONMENT

SPECIAL COMMITTEE ON
EQUAL OPPORTUNITIES

MEMBER
TRAFFIC & OFF STREET PARKING
REVENUE & TAXATION

January 27, 1978

Mr. Jerome O. Nelson
Administrative Assistant
Public Service Projects
Job Development Division
Office of Equal Opportunity/
  Affirmative Action
University of Southern California
Los Angeles, California 90007

Dear Mr. Nelson:

I'd like to recommend Raymond Washington for a
position as supervisor of a cleaning crew. Mr. Washington
is a most capable young man, physically able to do the
work and a proven leader in group situations. In fact,
one could note that he is particularly gifted in leadership skills, something that can only be an asset for a
position in which motivation and team production are
significant.

I appreciate your consideration on the matter.

Sincerely,

ROBERT FARRELL
Councilman, Eighth District

RF:djf

*Pic 8-23: Letter of recommendation from Robert Farrell, Councilman, Eighth District
recommending Raymond Washington be promoted to CETA
clean-up crew supervisor, dated 1-27-1978*

CHAPTER THIRTEEN
DECEPTION AND BETRAYAL

Ray Rhone explained, "Raymond was never about the money or the drugs, he was all about the power and the respect. Period." Raymond made a comment to Rhone about three or four weeks before he died that stuck with Rhone. "He had no idea how things in the Crips had got so out of control, it was never supposed to be like this, Crip against Crip. Raymond had lost control of the set. He said over and over that the Crips were supposed to be modeled after the Black Panthers, and they were organized to help the neighborhoods."

Court-certified gang identifier and expert witness Robert Walker found this hard to believe, and states on his website that, "These statements are all romantic folklore with absolutely no substance. Raymond was just a troubled fifteen-year-old kid who hung around other troubled fourteen and fifteen-year-old youths. Raymond had been kicked out of a number of schools, and had already been involved in the juvenile detention system. Raymond, at fifteen, did not have the maturity, or the vision to formulate these great ideological ideas (to try and emulate the BPP) and plans that some 'social experts' espouse."[65] Obviously everyone who actually knew Raymond Washington disagreed with this sentiment. It did start out that way, it just did not remain that way.

It was hard for me to imagine that Raymond could not have foreseen the eventual breakdown of the internal structure of the Crips. With all the internal planning and coordination, he had to realize that once he and Williams were locked up, there was no one left to lead the group. With no Robin-Hood-like leader, and no moral compass, the set's remaining leaders led through fear, brutality, and violence. Those qualities were already deeply ingrained into the gang's behavior, and in the streets of South Central Los Angeles. That was the Crip's culture whether Raymond chose to realize it or not. It could only escalate as each new generation came up on the streets, and tried to make their own name a legend.

Marcus Jones said again that he considered Raymond a friend, an ally, and that after Raymond had been released from prison he called on him for help. Marcus had taken up selling marijuana to make money, and had carved out his own small Crip set in the area around his home. He was known as the "go to" guy for pot until one day another set, the Hoover Crips, started to move into the neighborhood. They told people that they had to pay them a "tax" for protection from the other thugs in the neighborhood. Finally the day came when the Hoover Crips approached Marcus. He said they told him that they were moving into the neighborhood, and that he would have to pay a tax for protection of his small drug dealing business.

Marcus didn't know what to do at first, and then he remembered that he had heard that Raymond was out of prison. He set out in the city looking for him, and said it took a few days to finally locate Raymond. According to Marcus, "When Raymond went to prison, he was crazy and would do anything and go anywhere. He just had no fear of anything. But after he got out, he was quieter and not as crazy. He thought things through more and was not so quick to act."

Marcus told Raymond that he was being extorted and forced to pay a tax for his drug dealing business. He said Raymond was not happy that he was mixed up in dealing drugs, and that he expressed that loud and clear. Throughout all my interviews this point was made over and over, Raymond did not do drugs of any kind and rarely drank alcohol. He felt he had to always be ready for combat, and had to be sharp to survive. Raymond agreed to help Marcus out and sent out word that he wanted to meet the gang that was attempting to tax Marcus. A meeting was arranged with the Hoover

Crips. They agreed to meet at a power station on Figueroa Street. When Marcus and Raymond showed up, however, it felt like they were about to be ambushed by the Hoover Crip set. Raymond and Marcus took off and never made the meeting, but the taxes stopped being collected. Marcus said that happened in late 1978, and he moved to Inglewood shortly afterward. It was the last time Marcus would see Raymond Washington.

Tony Craddock recalled that, "Raymond had gone to Texas with his mother and was doing fine. If he had stayed out there, who knows, maybe he would have survived and be alive today, but no, he came back and found himself alone. He was like a man with no country, all the hood motherfuckers had grown up and got jobs and moved on and got on with their lives. And here Raymond is still hanging out at the high school doing that dumb shit. He was stuck in the past and life had passed him by. Shortly after that he was assassinated. After that, the real battles started in the neighborhood." This account conflicts with the documentation showing Raymond working as a supervisor for the City of Los Angeles, and the comments in those letters show that he had been working for several years. In fact, Raymond had moved on, at least partially. He was working a job and, according to Derard, "Had slowed his roll and was nearly completely out of the gang's affairs on the streets." (See Pic 8-7, 8-8)

However, I did interview Thomassine Crawford (aka Birdie), a cousin of Raymond Washington, who was several years younger than Raymond and also attended Fremont High School. Here is her recollection of Raymond in the last year of his life: "I had grown up within walking distance from Fremont High School. As I grew up, I heard the name Raymond Washington over and over again. Friends, neighbors, and family would recall stories they heard about him. The stories were so incredible that to me it seemed that he almost could not have been real. I remember thinking that he was just a made-up story because people needed a hero in the neighborhood. Then one day I found out Raymond Washington was my cousin! I was stunned. He was not only a real person; he was related to my family.

"Once day at Fremont, a bunch of girls showed up and tried to get into it with a friend of mine over a guy. It was 1978, and they were Criplettes, but I was not about to abandon my friend, so I defended her. They were really mad and went to Raymond, basically asking him for permission to come after me. When he asked who I was, what was my name, they told him and he said, 'No, that's my cousin. Leave her alone.' They showed up at my home one day, low riders filled the streets and there were a lot of them [Criplettes]. They said Raymond told them to tell me that I should stay out of the fight between the two girls (my friend and the Criplette). I said, no, I won't. Later I asked Raymond about their claim, and he told me he said to leave me alone. Nothing ever happened to me after that. Everyone left me alone." Clearly in 1978 Raymond was still very much involved in gang affairs, but, as he had done his entire life, he compartmentalized his life, allowing only certain people to see certain aspects of who he really was.

Another brief account that Thomassine recalled describes this compartmentalization very well. She remembered Raymond telling her grandmother (his paternal grandmother) that, "He had to change his ways and his life because he had a baby on the way." (See Pics 8-18, 8-19) She said that he went on and on about how he had a baby on the way and how it had changed his whole outlook. Except this would have been his second child. The first child was a son, Lil Ray—and was already a year or so old. (See Pics 8-14 through 8-17) This is yet another example of Raymond selectively telling specific people facts about his life, just enough that they felt included, but not enough to show the entire picture.

Thomassine also recalled seeing Raymond at the Fremont High School football games. She said, "I would go to the games and see Raymond walking past with his crew. He always had several people walking with him, and he would point at me and acknowledge me in the crowd. He was always watching out for me, he would even walk me to school in the morning, and make sure I got home safe when school was out. He was very, and I mean very, protective of me." Clearly Raymond was still involved in the Crips recruiting and calling the shots in 1978.

Thinking about this conversation with Thomassine Crawford, and also Tony Craddock's account of Raymond hanging around Fremont High School in 1978, I began to realize that Raymond was very much like a pro-athlete who has spent his entire early life preparing to make it into the big time. You see it time and time again in popular culture. An athlete makes it big, and achieves almost mythical status in their athletic achievements. Everyone knows their name, wherever they go they are recognized and loved. Then the day comes when they realize this is nearly over. They have worked their whole life to achieve this status and now it is nearly done. They are lost. Their whole identity is wrapped up in the sport. In Raymond's case, his whole identity was wrapped up in the Crips, and he could not find a way to walk away with dignity. (See Pics 8-11 through 8-13)

Additionally Marcus Jones' account of having to locate Raymond to help him out with the Hoover Crips that were trying to tax him shows that Raymond was no longer as involved with the gang affairs as he had been in the past. He was trying to regain control of the gang and roll all the warring sets into two major Crip gangs: The East side and The West side. He did not live to see that dream realized.

James Ward remembered the last time he saw Raymond. James was driving in the old neighborhood and saw him. Ward didn't know that Raymond was back in California. He called out to him, and Raymond turned around. When he recognized James, he smiled, and came over to the car. James recalled Raymond was alone at the time and said, "Raymond, why don't you have some bodyguards or something? You should not be out here alone!" and that Raymond had replied, 'Man, I don't need no bodyguards!' James believed that Raymond did not see himself the way everyone else did. "He just could not understand that there were people out there that would kill him." Raymond asked Ward if he wanted to hang out. Ward needed to get back to the West side. He took Raymond to get his car and that was the last time he saw Raymond Washington.

On August 9th at approximately 10 p.m., Raymond was staying with friends at 6326 South San Pedro in apartment #8 in Los Angeles. (See Pics 6-3, 6-4) A car drove up to the apartment building, and a voice called out to Raymond. Remember, Raymond had ingrained in his set to "never approach a car that you don't know or are not familiar with." According to Ricky Benjamin (now deceased), an eyewitness to the murder, "Raymond said he knew the car and approached the occupants. He asked who was in the car, constantly being cautious, and the occupants announced their names. Raymond smiled and walked to the car, unafraid."

Much like Achilles, the hero of the *Iliad*, Raymond had a weakness that his enemies had exploited. He valued loyalty and friendship over everything else. That value was used against him as he was called to the car by a familiar voice. He was met by a shotgun blast to the abdomen. The occupants then drove away. Ricky Benjamin said that Raymond told them he knew who the shooter was, and that he would take care of it as soon as he healed. Mentally he was not beaten, he would not, *could not* believe that he had received a fatal wound, and refused to disclose who had shot him.

Raymond died later that night, approximately one hour and twenty minutes after the shooting, at Morningside Hospital located at 8711 South Harvard Boulevard in Los Angeles, California. (See Pic 8-4) Ricky Benjamin told Derard Barton many years later, "That the memories of watching his friend and boyhood hero being shot had really messed him up. He had nightmares about it, and could not get the scene out of his mind."

Raphael Pattaway said, "It was crazy how Raymond died. He died by his own rules. He always said never walk up on a car and then he goes and breaks his own rules. I think though as he got older, he became complacent and that was why he walked up on that car and got killed. I think he knew who it was in the car, there is no question about that, in my mind. He knew them." Raphael was a block away when the shooting happened, and heard the gunshot.

Derard Barton described Raymond's funeral with a quiet and pain-filled voice. Tears began to form in his eyes some thirty-five years later as we talked at his job one night in Culver City, California. "It feels like it was yesterday. I was in Germany serving in the army when I was notified of Raymond's death. We were writing letters back and forth, and I asked him to stay out of the gangbanging. (See Pics 8-11 through 8-13) I had heard the streets were heating up, and I pleaded with him to stay out of it."

Derard recalled, "At the viewing there were several people who were armed and standing by Raymond's coffin, watching and waiting for anyone to start some shit. I was one of them, and we made damn sure that no one disrespected Raymond's funeral, or viewing." He continued, "When I came back for the funeral, it was an amazing sight. Low riders stopped traffic as the funeral procession made its way from the viewing to Raymond's final resting place in Lincoln Cemetery in Compton, California." According to Derard, and nearly every other person I interviewed for the book, the funeral procession looked like "the president had died, there were so many cars as people lined up to say goodbye to Raymond." (See Pics 7-1, 7-2)

There was no mention of his death in the *Los Angeles Times* or *The New York Times*, or any other major newspaper as there was when Stanley Williams died, but on the hardcore streets of South Central Los Angeles, Watts, and Compton, the slaying of Washington was akin to a presidential assassination.[3]

I traveled to Los Angeles twice in the spring of 2014 to do research on Raymond Washington, and to see the places he and Craig Craddock lived, where they went to school, and where they ultimately died. I drove all through Compton and Watts (See Pics 6-6 through 6-10), and visited both the Lincoln Cemetery where Raymond is buried and the Evergreen Cemetery where Craig Craddock is buried. (See Pic 7-6)

At the Lincoln Cemetery I looked row-by-row for Raymond Washington's grave, and was unable to find it. I returned the next day and asked the caretaker that was present if he could help me locate a gravesite. He laughed and replied, "I doubt it. We have over eight thousand graves here, but who are you looking for?" I told him Raymond Washington. He smiled and said, "Of course I know where Raymond's grave is, he gets visitors constantly." He walked in a direct line to a small, modest gravestone and said, "Here he is!" I asked about the visitors and if they received a lot of them for Raymond. He replied, "Yes, we do. A lot of people come and sit, talk, and then leave. Raymond is one of the most visited graves in the cemetery. He must have been something special because people keep coming, and he has been here a long, long time." (See Pics 7-3 through 7-5)

I looked around at other gravesites. Most were much more elaborate and ornate. Some were new, some were very old. I thought about what I had learned about Raymond Washington over the past year. I smiled and thought that this is the way Raymond would have wanted it. His grave wasn't flashy, and it was not gaudy. It was simple and direct, just like he was. Thirty-five or more years after his death, he is still most definitely remembered and visited often.

Another side of the lingering memory of Raymond Washington was best detailed by his daughter, Rayshana Washington. She is Raymond's youngest daughter and was born after his death. I was able to connect with her and get her thoughts on the father she never met. While we were speaking about Raymond, she relayed this experience she had one day in July of 2013, nearly thirty-five years after her father had been killed.

"I was participating in the California cease-fire, and I was at the 'Up-fest' and they had something in memory of Trayvon Martin.[66] There was this one particular guy there and he was a Blood, from the Blood side of the gangs, and we were walking around. I was wearing a shirt that I had made-up that has my father's photo screen-printed on the front. A guy came up to me and asked, 'Who is that on your shirt?' My friend, Skip, introduced me to him and said, 'This is Raymond Washington's youngest daughter.' I reached out to shake his hand and this man gave a look like I disgusted him. He did not want me to touch him! He gave me a look like Mmm, Mmm, Mmm. I was worried that something was about to happen because he looked at me with such hatred. I looked at Skip to see if I had done something wrong. He said, 'No.' I told Skip I wanted to go before something happened and that guy tried to do something to me, so we left. I asked Skip later what that was about. Skip said, 'Evidently he still has a lot of hatred in his heart for your father, who knows what your father did to him.'"

To me this spoke loud and clear that the memory of the dark side of who Raymond Washington was, and the things that he did, are also still alive and well in his enemies' memories today.

This was the reality of who Raymond Lee Washington was, both good and bad. He was the general in charge of thirty thousand soldiers. Brutal? Cunning? Sociopathic? Maybe, but necessary for survival. And, as any Crip will tell you, "Crippin ain't easy, but it is necessary."

CHAPTER FOURTEEN
SHADY AFTERMATH

The aftermath of Raymond's death can be described as nothing but open gang warfare on the streets of Los Angeles. People have made many claims about who was in charge of the Crips, and what kind of control any leader may have had over the organization. The statistical data is clear. These stats are taken from three websites and recall the murder rates before and after Raymond's death. Raymond died five days before his twenty-sixth birthday on August 9, 1979. The following year, Los Angeles would experience the single worst year in homicides per capita of any year before or since. (See below, 1980).[67] Raymond Washington's assassination did not go unanswered on the streets of Los Angeles.

Another newspaper article taken off the web describes the increase and that the FBI had no idea why the gang murder rate in Los Angeles had increased so drastically from 1970 to 1979. "In 1980 the rate of homicides had increased to 6 per day in Los Angeles and city officials are described as 'puzzled by the increase.'"[68]

It should also be noted that during the ten-year period of the rise of the Crips nation under the leadership of Raymond Washington from 1969-1979, Los Angeles suffered, "The largest ten year absolute increase (in the homicide rate—84.0%) which occurred from 1970 to 1979, when rates rose from 12.5 per 100,000 population to 23.0/100,000, nearly double the rate."

The CDC article continues: "Blacks and Hispanics were 5.6 and 2.3 times more likely, respectively, than white non-Hispanics to become homicide victims. Blacks were at greatest risk of victimization, with a rate of 45.6/100,000 population. The greatest absolute increase in homicide rates occurred among blacks, whose rates rose from 35.7/100,000 in 1970 to 61.3/100,000 in 1979. However, the highest percentage increase—over 166.7%—occurred among Hispanics, from 11.1 in 1970 to 29.6 in 1979."

FIGURE 2: HOMICIDES BY YEAR

YEAR	# OF HOMICIDES	YEAR	# OF HOMICIDES	YEAR	# OF HOMICIDES
1969	377	1988	736	2001	605
1970	491	1989	874	2002	646
1975	556	1990	983	2003	526
1978	627	1991	1,025	2004	515
1979	783	1992	1,092	2005	490
1980	**1,028**	1993	1,092	2006	478
1985	777	1994	850	2007	396
1986	831	1995	838	2008	382
1987	812	2000	542	2009	315

"The increasing homicide rate in Los Angeles during the 1970s can be attributed almost entirely to changes in homicide rates among black and Hispanic males (Figure 2, above). Rates for white non-Hispanic males were only slightly higher in the latter half of the decade than in the first half, and there was no consistent upward trend. The rates for white non-Hispanic, black, and Hispanic females did not change substantially.

"In 56.6% of homicides, victims were killed with some type of gun; handguns were used in 79.3% of these cases. In 23.3% of cases, cutting instruments were used; 10.6% of victims were bludgeoned to death; and 9.6% were killed by other means. Verbal arguments most commonly preceded homicides (32.7% of cases). During the 10-year period, 48.4% of homicides occurred in homes."[69]

After 1979 *The Journal of the American Medical Association* (JAMA) published a report on gang homicides in Los Angeles in 1995. Here are their findings: "A total of 7,288 gang-related homicides occurred in Los Angeles County from 1979 through 1994; 5541 of these homicides occurred in Los Angeles Police Department and Los Angeles County Sheriff's Department jurisdictions. During the study period, the proportion of all homicides that were gang related increased from 18.1% to 43.0% (P < .001). Of the 5541 gang-related homicide victims, 4580 (85.6%) were aged 15 to 34 years, 93.3% were African American or Hispanic, 5157 (93.2%) were male, 3559 (64.2%) were gang members, and 1408 (25.4%) occurred during drive-by shootings. Firearms were used in an increasing proportion of homicides, from 71.4% in 1979 to 94.5% in 1994. Homicides by semiautomatic handguns dramatically increased during the study period. Gang-related homicide rates for African-American males aged 15 to 19 years increased from 60.50 per 100,000 population per year in 1979 to 1981 to 192.41 per 100,000 population per year in 1989 to 1991.

"Gang-related homicides in Los Angeles County have reached epidemic proportions and are a major public health problem. To prevent gang violence, the root causes of violent street gang formation must be alleviated, the cycle of violent street gang involvement must be broken, and access to firearms must be limited."[70]

CHAPTER FIFTEEN

CRIP NATION TODAY

In ten years, the gang had grown from two sixteen-year-old kids talking on Raymond Washington's Mother's front porch about what to call their gang, to an estimated thirty thousand active Crip gang members. That is roughly the size of a very large infantry division in the U.S. Army.[71] Try to tell me that Raymond Washington did not strike a nerve with human psychology and sociology when he formed the Crips, especially when you grasp some countries in the world today do not have entire armies that large, and they are paid combatants.

Crips join, work, and die for no pay. Again, I cite Joseph Campbell and *The Power of Myth*. Raymond Washington and the Crip subculture filled a void in gang members' lives that they were willing to die for. By comparison, the Los Angeles Police Department had a total number of sworn personnel at approximately twelve thousand. It was then reduced to approximately eight thousand five hundred under Chief Gates.

By the mid-1990s, there were six hundred fifty thousand gang members in the U.S. and one hundred fifty thousand in Los Angeles County alone. Blood and Crip gang factions are found throughout the U.S. as well as abroad.[44]

According to the FBI, Crip gang members have served in every branch of the US military.[72] Who knew how big the Crips would become? No one could have predicted the explosive growth of the set, and the impact it would have on the entire world.

CRIPS MYTHS DEBUNKED

FALSE: The Crips started out as the Baby Avenue Cribs.

FALSE: The Crips gained the name the Crips after a senior gang member was shot in the leg and later always walked with a limp. (Law enforcement)

FALSE: The Crips got its name when its leader was shot in the leg and thereafter strutted around his turf with a cane. (*Time Magazine* interview with Lyle Joseph Thomas aka Joseph "Bartender" Thomas, 1975)

FALSE: Raymond Washington named the gang after a woman who was pushing a baby stroller down the street as they searched for a gang name and blurted out, "We will call ourselves the Cribs." (John "Moon" McDaniels)

FALSE: The Crips got the name from a football injury that Raymond Washington received. He had broken his leg playing football and was in a cast and walked with a limp afterward. (Marcus Jones)

TRUE: The Crips did not start out as the Baby Avenue Cribs. They started out as the Crips. The name came from a nickname that Raymond's older brother, Reggie, was given by band members of the Fremont High School band. Reggie was very bow legged. The kids would write their names on their shoes and Reggie wrote Crip on his. (Derard Barton)

FALSE: Raymond Washington was born in Texas. His mother then moved to Los Angeles. (Streetgangs.com) (*http://www.laweekly.com/2005-12-15/news/"tookie"-s-mistaken-identity/*)

TRUE: Raymond Washington was not born in Texas or Arizona. He was Born in Los Angeles at the Los Angeles County General Hospital. (See Appendix)

FALSE: Bunchy Carter helped Raymond Washington Start the Crips. (Bureau of Justice Assistance)

TRUE: Alprentice Bunchy Carter did not start the Crips with Raymond Washington. Carter was twenty-seven years old in 1969 when he died. Raymond was sixteen at that time. Bunchy Carter died January 16, 1969. Raymond Washington formed the Crips the next fall approximately in September/October of 1969, which was between eight and nine months after Bunchy Carter died. (*http://en.wikipedia.org/wiki/Bunchy_Carter*).

FALSE: Stanley "Tookie" William was the co-founder of the Crips. (*http://en.wikipedia.org/wiki/Stanley_"tookie"_Williams*)

TRUE: Stanley "Tookie" Williams did not start the Crips with Raymond Washington. Williams headed up the West side Crips of Los Angeles after he met Raymond and was "given the assignment" of the West side. He was a formidable gang member and leader but he was not the founder of the Crips.

TRUE: Raymond Washington formed the Crips at the age of sixteen, with his closest friend and ally Craig Craddock. According to associates, Craddock was the first of the original Crips to die. He died on October 5, 1972, two weeks after his eighteenth birthday. (Derard Barton)

FALSE: Stanley "Tookie" Williams was in the vehicle used to kill Raymond Washington and called to Raymond, shooting him in an attempt to take over the Crips. (*Gang Blogs*)

TRUE: Raymond Washington was not killed by Stanley "Tookie" Williams. Williams was incarcerated in jail at the time of Raymond's murder. Additionally, Williams did not order Raymond's murder.

FALSE: Raymond Washington picked the color blue for his gang the Crips because it was the school color of Fremont High School, the last school he attended. (John "Moon" McDaniels)

TRUE: Raymond picked the color to represent the Crips as blue. Not because it was the school colors of the last school he attended (Fremont High's colors are actually burgundy and gray) but because he wanted to set himself and the Crips apart from the Black Panthers. At the time, the Panthers used the term Blood (blood is red) to refer to each other. Additionally the Crips came up with the term "Cuz" to refer to fellow Crips after the term was frequently used by a West side Crip who went by the name "Buck." It was accepted and further set them apart from the Panthers and later the Bloods.

FALSE: Raymond Washington received a large scar on his face from a fight in prison. (*Gang Blogs*)

TRUE: Raymond was stabbed in prison but was barely grazed. (*Allhood Publications*) Verified with a family member of Raymond Washington.

TRUE: Raymond had a large scar on his face but not from a gang fight or from prison. He received it confronting a neighborhood kid who was watching him fight his older brother. They had been in an argument and after the fight was over Raymond approached the onlooker and said, "What the fuck are you looking at?" Out of fear, the kid lashed out with a knife and cut Raymond's left cheek. The cut was deep and required stitches. The kid was never seen again, his family got him out of L.A. that night. (Derard Barton)

FALSE: Crips co-founder Craig Craddock was killed by members of the Los Angeles Police Department. (*Allhood Publications*)

FALSE: Craig Craddock died of six gunshot wounds to the head and chest. (Tony Craddock/Marcus Jones)

TRUE: Craig Craddock was killed by Steve, a guy that he tormented, humiliated, and robbed. He spit in Steve's face after Steve told him he had a gun and to leave him alone, or he would kill him. Steve then shot him twice in the chest, killing him instantly in October 1972. (see Craig Craddock's death certificate)

BOOK AND RESOURCE REFERENCES

Allhood Publications, 90003. Volume 3. Issue 5, Apr–Jun 2008.

Bakeer, Donald. *The Original South Central L.A. Crips.* Precocious Publishing Co., 1999.

Barnett, Vic, and Toby Lewis. *Outliers in Statistical Data.* Vol. 3. New York: Wiley, 1994.

Campbell, Joseph, and Bill Moyers. *The Power of Myth.* Random House LLC, 2011.

Crips and Bloods: Made in America, directed by Stacy Peralta. 2009. Los Angeles., CA: New Video Group, Inc. Docuramafilms. DVD.

Davis, Greg "Batman." *Original Gangster.* Schiffer, 2012.

Howell, James C., and John P. Moore. *History of Street Gangs in the United States.* U.S. Department of Justice, Bureau of Justice Assistance [and] Office of Juvenile Justice and Delinquency Prevention, 2010.

Hutson, H. Range; Deirdre Anglin; Demetrios N. Kyriacou; Joel Hart; and Kelvin Spears. "The Epidemic of Gang-related Homicides in Los Angeles County from 1979 through 1994." *JAMA* 274, No. 13 (1995): 1031-1036.

Irwin, John. *Lifers: Seeking Redemption in Prison*. Routledge, 2010.

Gladwell, Malcolm. *Outliers: The Story of Success*. Penguin UK, 2008.

Lords of the Mafia: Gangsta King: Raymond Lee Washington. Narrated by Robert Stack. PBS Special. 7/5/2004.

Roberts, Wess. *Victory Secrets of Attila the Hun*. Random House LLC, 2012.

Roberts, Wess. *Leadership Secrets of Attila the Hun*. Hachette Book Group, 2007.

Sloan, Cle "Bone." *Bastards of the Party* [Motion picture]. New York: Home Box Office (2007). DVD.

Steinbeck, John. *The Grapes of Wrath*. Penguin, 2006.

Tzu, Sun. *The Art of War*. Translated by Thomas Cleary. *Shambhala, Boston* (1988).

Valdez, Al. *Gangs: A Guide to Understanding Street Gangs*. Law Tech Publishing Company, 1998.

Williams, Stanley Tookie. *Blue Rage, Black Redemption: A Memoir*. Simon and Schuster, 2007.

APPENDIX III
ENDNOTES

1. Woods, Cliff. Personal communications with Fortier, Zach. Various dates 2012-2014. (page 11)

2. Warren, Jenifer, and Dolan, Maura. "Tookie Williams Is Executed." Local page of *Los Angeles Times*. Dec 13, 2005. http://www.latimes.com/local/la-me-execution13dec13,0,3684934.story#axzz2y82CGoSh (page 11)

3. Krikorian, Michael. "Tookie's Mistaken Identity, On the Trail of the Real Founder of the Crips." *LAWeekly News*. Dec 15, 2005. http://www.laweekly.com/2005-12-15/news/tookie-s-mistaken-identity/ (pages 11, 58, 60, 105, 107)

4. "The Nation: Portrait of a Gang Leader." *Time Magazine*. June 30, 1975. http://content.time.com/time/subscriber/article/0,33009,917567,00.html (page 12)

5. "Julius Caesar." Wikipedia. http://en.wikipedia.org/wiki/Julius_Caesar (page 13)

6. "Raymond Washington." Wikipedia. http://en.wikipedia.org/wiki/Raymond_Washington (pages 13, 38)

7. "10 Famous Cases of Unsolved Murder & Mystery." *The List Blog–Top 10*. http://www.listzblog.com/top_ten_unsolved_murders_mysteries_list.html (page 13)

8. "Cold Case: 20 Biggest Unsolved Murders." *The Writer's Forensics Blog*. http://writersforensicsblog.wordpress.com/2010/05/23/cold-case-20-biggest-unsolved-murders-cross-post/ (page 13)

9. "The Crips." Wikipedia. http://en.wikipedia.org/wiki/The_Crips (page 13)

10. Howell, James C., and Moore, John P. *History of Street Gangs in the United States*. US Department of Justice, Bureau of Justice Assistance [and] Office of Juvenile Justice and Delinquency Prevention, 2010. (page 14)

11. "Heredity and Environment." Wikipedia. http://en.wikipedia.org/wiki/Heredity_and_environment (page 19)

12. "Watts Riots." Wikipedia. http://en.wikipedia.org/wiki/Watts_Riots (page 20)

13. Dawsey, Darrell. "To CHP Officer Who Sparked Riots, It Was Just Another Arrest. Watts: Then and Now." *Los Angeles Times*. August 19, 1990. Accessed February 6, 2015. http://articles.latimes.com/1990-08-19/local/me-2790_1_chp-officer (page 23)

14. Lee, Hatty. "Remembering the 1965 Watts Riots." *ColorLines*. August 14, 2010. Accessed February 6, 2015. http://colorlines.com/archives/2010/08/watts_riots.html (page 25)

15. A report by the Governor's commission on the Los Angeles Riots. "144 Hours in August 1965." Part 4 of *Violence in the City—An End or a Beginning?* http://www.usc.edu/libraries archives/cityinstress/mccone/part4.html (page 25)

16. *Watts Riots*. PBS. A Huey P. Newton Story. http://www.pbs. org/hueypnewton/times/times_watts.html (page 26)

17. "White Front." Wikipedia. http://en.wikipedia.org/wiki/ White_Front (page 26)

18. "Incursion." Dictionary.com. http://dictionary.reference. com/browse/incursion (page 26)

19. "Bayonet." Dictonary.com. http://dictionary.reference.com/ browse/bayonet (page 27)

20. Cosgrove, Ben. "The Fire Last Time: Life in Watts, 1966." *Time*. November 20, 2014. Accessed February 6, 2015. http:// time.com/3640068/the-fire-last-time-life-in-watts-1966/ (page 28)

21. "Watts Riots." *Civil Rights Digital Library*. Last modified: November 20, 2013. http://crdl.usg.edu/events/watts_ri- ots/?Welcome&Welcome&Welcome (page 28)

22. "I Only Meant To Get My Feet Wet." The Whispers, 1972. https://www.youtube.com/watch?v=_5lTmBY2FlM (page 31)

23. "Seems Like I Gotta Do Wrong." The Whispers, 1970. https:// www.youtube.com/watch?v=W7e691r7pQM&feature=kp (page 31)

24. "Run Away Child, Running Wild." The Temptations, 1969. https://www.youtube.com/watch?v=n3uNRGScc3I (page 31)

25. "It's The Way Nature Planned It." The Four Tops, 1972. https://www.youtube.com/watch?v=PVQ9f_l6e_o (page 31)

26. "Roger E. Mosley." Wikipedia. http://en.wikipedia.org/wiki/ Roger_E._Mosley (page 32)

27. "The Official Malcolm X Biography." http://www.malcolmx. com/about/bio.html (page 34)

28. Drash, Wayne. "Malcolm X Killer Freed After 44 Years." *CNN.* April 28, 2010. Accessed February 6, 2015. http://www.cnn.com/2010/CRIME/04/26/malcolmx.killer/ (page 34)

29. "Bunchy Carter." Wikipedia. http://en.wikipedia.org/wiki/Bunchy_Carter (page 34)

30. "John Huggins." Wikipedia. http://en.wikipedia.org/wiki/John_Huggins (page 35)

31. Morales, Gabe. "Crips." *Gang Prevention Services.* http://www.gangpreventionservices.org/Crips.asp (pages 36, 43)

32. "5 Most Unjust Convictions Of Black Men That Were Overturned." *NewsOne for Black America.* July 12, 2011. http://newsone.com/1373205/exonerated-black-men-released-from-prison/ (page 36)

33. *Crips and Bloods: Made in America.* DVD. Directed by Stacy Peralta. 2009; Los Angeles, CA: New Video Group, Inc. Docuramafilms. Accessed February 6, 2015. http://www.amazon.com/Crips-Bloods-America-Forest-Whitaker/dp/B002HLVMG6 (page 37, 42, 68)

34. Michael Conception interviewed by Mo'Nique. "The Mo'Nique Show Guest Rewind: Michael Conception Interview," *Bet.com* video, 6:10, July 15, 2010. http://www.bet.com/video/themoniqueshow/guestrewind/michael-conception-07-15-10-229119.html (page 68) (Author's note: Correct spelling of last name is Concepcion and not Conception as noted in title/link)

35. Barrett, Beth, and Kandel, Jason. "L.A. Gang History Runs Deep: Terror in our Streets." A special report on gang violence in Southern California. *The Los Angeles Daily-News.com.* September 26, 2004. http://lang.dailynews.com/socal/gangs/articles/ALL_p1side1.asp (page 43)

36. Sandman personal communications with Fortier, Zach. Various dates. (page 43, 70)

37. "Hearsay evidence." Merriam-Webster.com. http://www.merriam-webster.com/dictionary/hearsay+evidence?-show=0&t=1397421985 (page 44)

38. "Witness." Merriam-Webster.com. http://www.merriam-web-ster.com/dictionary/witness (page 44)

39. "Founder." The Learners Dictionary. http://www.learners-dictionary.com/definition/founder (page 53)

40. "Snoop Dogg—Drop It Like It's Hot ft. Pharrell Williams." *YouTube* video, 4:25. Posted by "SnoopDoggVEVO," December 24, 2009. http://youtu.be/GtUVQei3nX4?list=RDGtU-VQei3nX4 (page 56)

41. "Ice Cube C Walk." *YouTube* video, 0:31. Posted by "Der-rtyB22687," June 25, 2006. http://youtu.be/gREIBeiXgak (page 56)

42. "Original Westside Crips Talk About Being Convicted of Murder 40 Years Ago." *Streetgangs.com*. August 6, 2013. Accessed February 6, 2015 http://www.streetgangs.com/fea-tures/080613-original-Crips-robert-ballou#sthash.h4SU-CReL.HBZLmi3Q.dpuf (page 59)

43. "Founding member." LearnersDictionary.com. http://www.learnersdictionary.com/definition/founding%20member (page 60)

44. "Crips and Bloods: Made in America." *PBS.org*. Video. Directed by Stacy Peralta. 2009. Posted by "Independent Television Service." April 21, 2009. http://www.pbs.org/independen-tlens/cripsandbloods/film.html (page 60)

45. "Greatest Generation. Our Grandparents Were Heroes Once." WWII Museum on Tumblr. http://greatestgeneration.tum-blr.com/post/3794260978/private-james-clark-was-only-13-when-he-joined-the#.U5DrI_ldXNl (page 69)

46. "Calvin Graham." Wikipedia. http://en.wikipedia.org/wiki/Calvin_Graham (page 69)

47. "Jack Lucas Dies at 80; Earned Medal of Honor at 17." *The New York Times*. U.S. Section by the Associated Press. June, 2008. http://www.nytimes.com/2008/06/06/us/06lucas.html?_r=1& (page 69)

48. "Audie Murphy." Wikipedia. http://en.wikipedia.org/wiki/Audie_Murphy (page 70)

49. Snoop personal communications with Fortier, Zach. Various dates. (page 71)

50. Valdemar, Richard. "History of the Florence 13 Gang." *Gangs Blog*. Posted September 12, 2007. Accessed on Police, *The Law Enforcement Magazine*. February 6, 2015. http://www.policemag.com/blog/gangs/story/2007/09/history-of-the-florence-13-gang.aspx (page 81)

51. "Leadership Style." *The Wall Street Journal*. US Edition. Lessons in Leadership. Adapted from Murray, Alan. Harper Business. http://guides.wsj.com/management/developing-a-leadership-style/how-to-develop-a-leadership-style/ (page 86)

52. "Inside Bloods And Crips LA Gangs Documentary." *YouTube* video, 45:23. Posted by "Drugs War Documentary," November 28, 2012. http://youtu.be/zl3QhUHDM90 (page 93)

53. *Bastards of the Party*. DVD. Directed by Cle "Bone" Sloan. 2007; New York City: NY. *Home Box Office Inc.* (page 104)

54. Woods, Jonathan. "Inside LA's Drive-thru (and bulletproof) Funeral Home." *NBC News*. February 9, 2012. Accessed February 6, 2015. http://photoblog.nbcnews.com/_news/2012/02/09/10362637-inside-las-drive-thru-and-bulletproof-funeral-home (page 104)

55. "Tookie Williams." *YouTube* video, 0:30. Posted by "martha2065," August 23, 2011. http://youtu.be/Ewd4jvf5Fn4 (page107)

56. Gann, Brian. "The Crips (1971? -)." *BlackPast.org.* Remembered & Reclaimed. http://www.blackpast.org/aaw/crips-1971 (page 108)

57. "Crips." HIDTA. *Gangs.org.* http://gangs.umd.edu/Gangs/Crips.aspx (page 108)

58. "Secobarbital." Wikipedia. http://en.wikipedia.org/wiki/Secobarbital (page 115)

59. "Iliad." Wikipedia. http://en.wikipedia.org/wiki/Iliad (page 126)

60. Cartwright, Mark. "Achilles." *Ancient History Encyclopedia.* September 29, 2012. Accessed February 6, 2015. http://www.ancient.eu.com/achilles/ (page 128)

61. Rubin, Joel. "LAPD Officers Tampered With In-car Recording Equipment, Records Show." *Los Angeles Times.* April 7, 2014. Accessed February 6, 2015. http://articles.latimes.com/2014/apr/07/local/la-me-lapd-tamper-20140408 (page 129)

62. "Allhood Publications—Raymond Washington." *YouTube* video, 2:41. Posted by "CrippinTV," February 6, 2010. http://youtu.be/pjl9tvIVjL4 (page 130)

63. "Rosey Grier." Wikipedia. http://en.wikipedia.org/wiki/Rosey_Grier (page 133)

64. "Comprehensive Employment and Training Act." Wikipedia. http://en.wikipedia.org/wiki/Comprehensive_Employment_and_Training_Act (page 134)

65. Walker, Robert. "Crips and Bloods History." A first hand account of their real history and the myths surrounding the origin and founders of the gangs. March, 2014. http://www.gangsorus.com/Crips_bloods_history.htm (page 155)

66. "Welcome to the United In Peach Foundation." Accessed February 6, 2015. http://upfest.org/ (page 162)

67. "LA Homicides: 1970 to 2009. It's Getting Better All The Time." (Blog.) *City-Data.com.* July 3, 2010. http://www.city-data.com/forum/los-angeles/1021092-la-homicides-1970-2009-its-getting.html#ixzz33saa4gob (page 163)

68. "Los Angeles Murder Rate Soars." *N.Y. Times News Service.* July, 1980. http://news.google.com/newspapers?nid=1454&-dat=19800721&id=-lFIAAAAIBAJ&sjid=QBMEAAAAIBA-J&pg=4813,4294356 (page 163)

69. "Homicide—Los Angeles, 1970-1979." CDC. *MMWR Weekly.* Feb, 1986, 35(5); 61-5. http://www.cdc.gov/mmwr/preview/mmwrhtml/00000841.htm (page 164)

70. Hutson, H.R., Anglin, D., Kyriacou, D.N., Hart, J., Spears K. "The Epidemic of Gang-related Homicides in Los Angeles County from 1979 through 1994." *JAMA* 274 (1995):1031–1036. Accessed February 6, 2015. http://www.ncbi.nlm.nih.gov/pubmed/7563453 (page 165)

71. "Division (military)." Wikipedia. http://en.wikipedia.org/wiki/Division (page 166)

72. "2011 National Gang Threat Assessment—Emerging Trends." *The FBI Reports & Publications.* http://www.fbi.gov/stats-services/publications/2011-national-gang-threat-assessment (page 167)

ACKNOWLEDGMENTS

No project of this type can be completed without a lot of help and trust from the people who consented to being interviewed and questioned. It would still be a book that should have been written and a truth that has never been told if it were not for the following people: Violet Samuel, Derard Barton, Cliff Woods, James Ward, Marcus Jones, Raphael "Raphy" Pattaway, John "Moon" McDaniels, Tony Craddock, Ray Rhone, Thomassine "Birdie" Crawford, Rayshana Washington, Jason Tafoya, Travis Elliot, and Mike "S" aka Snoop.

My personal support system includes Blue Harvest Creative, SteeleShark Press, and Sally Herrick Harrington. Without them none of the books would be where they are today.

Special thanks to my wife Christina for putting up with the place this book mentally took me back to, staying by my side, and seeing it through.

Z.

Zach Fortier was a police officer for over thirty years specializing in K-9, SWAT, gangs, domestic violence, and sex crimes as an investigator. He has written five books about his life in police work. *CurbChek* won the bronze medal for True Crime in the 2013 Readers' Favorite International Book Awards. *Street Creds* and *Curbchek Reload* won a gold and silver medal respectively for True Crime in the 2014 Readers' Favorite International Book Awards.

His other works are *Hero To Zero*, which details the incredibly talented cops that he worked with that ended up going down in flames, some ended up in prison and one on the FBI's ten most wanted list. *Landed on Black* described the toxic culture of the police department and streets, ultimately leading to the realization that Zach has been afflicted with PTSD.

If you are looking for gritty, true crime stories, be sure to check out all of Zach Fortier's novels. Zach currently lives in the mountains of Colorado, with his wife Christina.

Made in the USA
Las Vegas, NV
19 October 2023

79383377R00111